Editor-in-Chief and Founder:
  Lyndon H. LaRouche, Jr.
Editorial Board: *Lyndon H. LaRouche, Jr. , Helga
  Zepp-LaRouche, Paul Gallagher, Tony Papert,
  Gerald Rose, Dennis Small, Jeffrey Steinberg,
  William Wertz*
Co-Editors: *Paul Gallagher, Tony Papert*
Managing Editor: *Nancy Spannaus*
Technology: *Marsha Freeman*
Books: *Katherine Notley*
Ebooks: *Richard Burden*
Graphics: *Alan Yue*
Photos: *Stuart Lewis*
Circulation Manager: *Stanley Ezrol*

INTELLIGENCE DIRECTORS
Counterintelligence: *Jeffrey Steinberg, Michele
  Steinberg*
Economics: *John Hoefle, Marcia Merry Baker,
  Paul Gallagher*
History: *Anton Chaitkin*
Ibero-America: *Dennis Small*
Russia and Eastern Europe: *Rachel Douglas*
United States: *Debra Freeman*

INTERNATIONAL BUREAUS
Bogotá: *Miriam Redondo*
Berlin: *Rainer Apel*
Copenhagen: *Tom Gillesberg*
Houston: *Harley Schlanger*
Lima: *Sara Madueño*
Melbourne: *Robert Barwick*
Mexico City: *Gerardo Castilleja Chávez*
New Delhi: *Ramtanu Maitra*
Paris: *Christine Bierre*
Stockholm: *Ulf Sandmark*
United Nations, N.Y.C.: *Leni Rubinstein*
Washington, D.C.: *William Jones*
Wiesbaden: *Göran Haglund*

ON THE WEB
e-mail: eirns@larouchepub.com
www.larouchepub.com
www.executiveintelligencereview.com
www.larouchepub.com/eiw
Webmaster: *John Sigerson*
Assistant Webmaster: *George Hollis*
Editor, Arabic-language edition: *Hussein Askary*

EIR (ISSN 0273-6314) *is published weekly
(50 issues), by EIR News Service, Inc.,
P.O. Box 17390, Washington, D.C. 20041-0390.
(703) 777-9451*

European Headquarters: E.I.R. GmbH, Postfach
Bahnstrasse 9a, D-65205, Wiesbaden, Germany
Tel: 49-611-73650
Homepage: http://www.eirna.com
e-mail: eirna@eirna.com
Director: Georg Neudecker

Montreal, Canada: 514-461-1557

Denmark: EIR - Danmark, Sankt Knuds Vej 11,
basement left, DK-1903 Frederiksberg, Denmark.
Tel.: +45 35 43 60 40, Fax: +45 35 43 87 57. e-mail:
eirdk@hotmail.com.

Mexico City: EIR, Sor Juana Inés de la Cruz 242-2
Col. Agricultura C.P. 11360
Delegación M. Hidalgo, México D.F.
Tel. (5525) 5318-2301
eirmexico@gmail.com

Canada Post Publication Sales Agreement
#40683579

Postmaster: Send all address changes to *EIR*, P.O.
Box 17390, Washington, D.C. 20041-0390.

Signed articles in *EIR* represent the views of the
authors, and not necessarily those of the Editorial
Board.

Depose
The Nazi Queen!

Murder on the Queen's Orders

July 16—It was Queen Elizabeth II personally, who ordered German Finance Minister Schäuble's virtual murder of the nation of Greece in Eurozone debt-summit negotiations over July 12-13.

The Greek debt negotiations had been proceeding in June. Germany's demands against Greece were much more moderate at that time, according to an AP wire of today carried in the *New York Times*. But then, those negotiations were adjourned on June 26, to await the results of the Greek referendum which was held on July 5. (In that referendum, Greeks overwhelmingly rejected the austerity demands of Germany and the Eurozone countries.)

Now during just the same period the negotiations were interrupted, Britain's Queen Elizabeth made a rare state visit to Germany over June 23-26, and met there with Chancellor Angela Merkel, among others. It is not known at this time whether she also met with German Finance Minister Wolfgang Schäuble. But on June 25, during the Queen's visit, Chancellor Merkel complained that Greek negotiations had "lost ground," and Schäuble warned that the sides were moving apart.

Then, last Saturday, July 11, on the eve of the summit which resumed the broken-off negotiations, Schäuble and the German delegation showed up with new demands, the "toughest ever," which even their allies said "came out of the blue," AP reports. One summit participant "said that the extra demands were immediately perceived as provocative." Schäuble had received and carried out the Queen's orders. He even demanded that Greece be thrown out of the eurozone. Although Greece was not thrown out at that time, the violations of sovereignty and genocidal conditions were so brutal that they amounted to Greece's murder.

"This makes it very clear," Lyndon LaRouche said today. "Schäuble is barking for the Queen."

Yet Schäuble was still insisting on a Greek exit from the Euro today, even after Greece had signed on to his diktat. "And he's going to get the exit he wants," said LaRouche. "It's obvious he's going to get an exit. And that's when Greece will go to Russia. And once they go to Russia, at that point what will happen is that the European continental region will go into a spin-dive

Chancellor Angela Merkel (right) receives Queen Elizabeth II in Berlin, June 26, 2015.

downward. And that will then shape everything.

"This is where the British are counting on Obama, to set forth a *casus belli*, which will actually be a British *casus belli*. Saving the situation will be the pretext for the war. Russia will get an ultimatum: either you submit to us, or we will go to war with you. The British will create a confrontation between Russia and the Presidency of the United States, and Obama, the President of the United States, will go to war with Russia.

"That's the scenario. And the game against China, is part of the same pattern. The case is clear. The question is: who's got the guts to face the reality? And there are very few people who have the guts to face that reality. Because, what's going to happen, is that suddenly the institutions of the United States government, will then launch war.

"What Schäuble has done on the Queen's orders, will be part of the pretext. The British Empire's policy will be, then, to get the United States to launch warfare against Russia. For which Russia will be prepared. It means the extermination of much of the human species, but the British Empire wants to reduce much of the human population anyway.

"But that's the reality. Let's see what kinds of guts and brains people may have. Because there's nothing else we can do beyond that. We've got to make that the challenge," LaRouche concluded.

EIR Contents

www.larouchepub.com Volume 42, Number 29, July 24, 2015

Cover This Week

Queen Elizabeth, at age 7 and today

I. WHAT IS OUR MISSION REALLY?

4 What Is Our Mission Really?
Lyndon LaRouche Addresses the Manhattan Project, July 18, 2015

20 A Turn of the Key in the Presidential Campaign
by Daniel Burke

II. MUSICAL INTERLUDE

23 Music Is Not Notes, It's the (In)Tension
by Lyndon H. LaRouche, Jr.

27 Max Planck and the Principle of Human Discovery in Music
by Caroline Hartmann

III. LONDON'S WORLD RULE THROUGH ASSASSINATION AND WAR

32 For Human Progress, Destroy the British Empire
The remarks of Jeffrey Steinberg and Jason Ross, excerpted from the July 17 LaRouche PAC webcast

42 The Murder of Greece: A Mystery We'd Better Solve
by Paul Gallagher

45 Greek Parliament Head: No to Blackmail!

46 The Financial System Is Bankrupt: The Only Salvation Is Glass-Steagall
by Helga Zepp-LaRouche

What Is Our Mission Really?

Saturday, July 18, 2015

Dennis Speed: My name is Dennis Speed, and on behalf of the LaRouche Political Action Committee, I want to welcome everybody here today. Two individuals are in New York City today: Barack Obama is downtown watching a hip-hop Broadway play about Alexander Hamilton, and here with us, is Lyndon LaRouche. [applause]

We had an eventful week, and we're going to go right to our Q&A, so that we have an opportunity for everybody to figure out how to help LaRouche do what he's trying to get done. Let's go right to the first question, here at the microphone.

Q: Hi Lyn. My question is around Glass-Steagall. Dennis just mentioned a number of things have happened this week. You had the intervention around Hillary's speech; then the subsequent rally. Four Senators, of course, are holding their ground so far, with Sanders just joining in now, in terms of his support for Glass-Steagall. At this point, anyway, Hillary Clinton seems to aligning with the White House; and I haven't read the latest reports from the organization in terms of the Wall Street reaction, but I'm assuming there's a big freakout going on, and a big panic of sorts.

My question to you is, what type of reaction should we continue to expect from this crowd? What's the next phase for us, now, after a week of activities in our deployments? And how would this lead to the impeachment of Barack Obama?

Lyndon LaRouche: Well, the situation now is that Obama is really bringing us to the edge of a thermonuclear confrontation. Now that's generally been the direction of his intentions; because everything he's done is in terms of the attack on Russia, in particular, which is what his focus point is,— because Russia is selected by the British monarchy, the British Empire, and by Wall Street, essentially is opposed to it, in this process. So there is a preparation in the direction of going toward an actual, general thermonuclear war, in which the British interests, represented by Obama, in the planet would be going after a general war throughout much of the planet. This would be coming very fast; it would happen almost in an instant; we're getting down to a question of actually instants, between what is the point between Russia's holding back on its ability to fight, and the launching of the actual war by Obama in particular, but essentially by the whole British Empire system. Because it's the British Empire system, which brought Obama into popularity, shall we say: that is the problem here.

So, our problem is to understand this, and to catch up on what this is all about. Now, the proper way to look at this thing is, don't look at this as some kind of audio/video whatever. Don't treat it that way.

What happens is, when that thing is ready to go, and the U.S. side, British side, starts to move, the move by

Federation of American Scientists

"On the edge of thermonuclear war:" Once developed, this B61-12 bomb would be the world's first guided nuclear gravity bomb, and, when deployed to Europe, would be a significant upgrade of NATO's nuclear capability—and, in the Russians' view, intention.

Russia will be very brief,—a very brief interval between the launching of the war, and Russia's response. Russia's point is not to become itself involved as the provoker of thermonuclear war, but to leave that job, shall we say, to the British Empire in general, and to Obama in particular. That's the intention.

We don't know how fast that will come; there are many factors in this thing. The idea of very precise calculations in this kind of thing is really wrong. There are points at which the "go" goes, and the followup action goes similarly. But there is no real plan, that we can precalculate on our side.

So we have to understand, we're into a situation where we're on the edge of a thermonuclear war, and where Germany would be on the edge of this thing, but Russia will be the defending party. The British Empire and Obama will be the aggressive party. That much is clear.

Now, obviously there are certain things that can happen, which would change some of these things, but this is what we've got. Because you don't have a perfect conclusion as to what the actions are going to be. But we have a very good estimate of what the nature of the action will be.

Now, of course, if Obama is removed from office, then this would probably prevent the actual launching of a thermonuclear war. And the best estimate is, that if Obama were removed from the Presidency, the war might not be launched. Because people in our government, in the U.S. government, would not want this war. Some people, yes, around Obama and so forth, yes. But the people, the responsible institutions of the United States, *do not want a thermonuclear war*, particularly one launched from the United States under the direction of the British Empire.

So that's where we stand, and there are lots of things we can do, to respond to this. There are no simple mechanisms of predetermined conditions which operate under these kinds of conditions. You've come into an area where the probability is acute, and you try to work from the probability, to handle the countdown which might lead to an actual warfare situation.

Q: My name is S— from New Jersey. You just answered all my questions on that. But I want to know, if the military from the United States and people who are in here with any sanity, would back Obama, or just tell him to buzz off? I just want to know if the military would have enough sense, *not* to go, and fight the Rus-

sians? You think they'd stand up and tell Obama where to go. I would, if I was still in.

What Happened to Hillary?

LaRouche: [laughs] Well, I would say, in response to that, that we have a role in this. In other words, we're not spectators; if we are spectators, we're idiots. Our job is to understand the way in which we can influence the process. For example, let's take what happened to Hillary Clinton. And this is a fun kind of thing, but this is typical of the way history really works: Now, we had one of our members there, when Hillary was giving the

---

The precedent is, as this little incident demonstrates out of Manhattan, that the situation is never predetermined completely. There are always the possibilities of interventions, impromptu or pre-prepared, which may change the whole course of events.

---

address. And at the end of that process, where she was gasping out the closure of what she had to say, our representative who was there, just as an observer, said, "Yes, what about Glass-Steagall?" And he repeated the statement, recapitulating it. She said nothing; she froze.

But the result was an immediate reaction through the audience and people like that, and so the thing very quickly spun out, becoming a national case. I mean, this is really one of the things, where a single statement, or a single pair of statements, from an observer, to a large audience, causes everything to go off but the fireworks. But this is quite useful. But the reaction was even more indicative: that people realized this was idiocy; that her policy which she expressed by the way she managed to bring her statement to a conclusion, proved that she was not fit to be a Presidential candidate of the United States at this time. And that's the essential thing.

Now therefore, the precedent is, as this little incident demonstrates out of Manhattan, that the situation is never predetermined completely. There are always the possibilities of interventions, impromptu or pre-prepared, which may change the whole course of events. And in a certain sense, that's exactly what happened in Manhattan, by the immediate close of her address.

So therefore, all of these kinds of situations are possible up to the very last possible moment,—that is, serious things are possible. And the importance is, to have a population which responds in such a way that it, the population in concern, actually is prepared to make a reasonable, and convincing intervention, in the process of what is threatened to be a thermonuclear warfare.

Q: Hi Lyndon, this is Daniel Burke. I feel very fortunate that I was able to be at that moment earlier this week, and that it simply was not possible to stay silent, as the opportunity presented itself.

But my question is about how the advances of the BRICS nations, how—I'm thinking about the 600 or 700 million young people in India, who suddenly are extraordinarily optimistic. And I'm thinking about the

---

If you look at the history of warfare, of modern major warfare, you'll see that even in the Eighteenth-Century, Nineteenth-Century levels, the element of surprise is crucial. And what is wrong with what most people think, is that they think that the surprise is not going to occur.

15-year-old in China, whose whole life has been characterized by huge progress. And at the same time, I'm reflecting on the horrible degeneration in the United States population, and in the young people, especially, that we intend to fight to organize to a higher level. So I guess I'm asking about—I know that there's been a huge advance in the creative powers of man in the BRICS process; and what can be done, how does that affect our ability to prevent the war from happening? How does that affect our ability to advance the United States population, who are so far behind at this point?

LaRouche: Look, the first thing is to consider the standpoint of warfare, because this is what we're up against. The important thing is to prevent the kind of warfare which is being threatened now. Or to prevent the kinds of actions which could lead into the activation of such a form of warfare.

Because warfare on a continental, transcontinental level, is not something that you can control once it starts. It has a logic of its own. If you look at the history of warfare, of modern major warfare, you'll see that even in the Eighteenth-Century, Nineteenth-Century levels, the element of surprise is crucial. And what is wrong with what most people think, is that they think that the surprise is not going to occur. That it will be a preplanned attack, by calculable forces, and in the course of most warfare, there are certain things, as a

larger process, that can influence the process which happens.

But in the particular case, where something has broken out, just like what happened with Hillary,—Hillary decided to muff it, and there was somebody in the audience who was ready to say "what about Glass-Steagall? What about Glass-Steagall?" And what happened was, the unexpected happened! It happened because there was a predetermination to do something good, as a single individual with friends, of course, in the environment, which changed the course of history!

And this is always the factor you have to keep in mind. I, of course, have been through this for a long time, because I've been operating in operations for most of my life, and it's a very long life by most people's standards. But the point is, there is no predetermined plan, which cannot be, as we say, "screwed up," as what happened to Hillary. She had no expectation of finding that thing; but what she did by not responding, *she lost her chance of becoming a Presidential candidate in full.*

Q: Good afternoon, I have one question for you: Do you have any news on Greece and Iran to share with us this afternoon?

LaRouche: Yes, something. That Greece has been butchered. Now, of course, the danger of this butchering of Greece, which has happened, was a possibility all the way through. It was a question, what would the British Empire do? And what happened in point of fact was that the British Empire intervened in the situation, to bring about the sequence of events.

In other words, what happened was, you had a situation that was ready. Schäuble in Germany was ready to do the job. But then, what happened, the Queen of England made two interventions into Germany in that context: The first time was to propose, simply, "well, let's explode it, let's kill it." So the British Empire, or the Queen herself, personally, intervened, to cause the Germans in particular, particularly Schäuble and Merkel, but Schäuble is most prominent in this thing, to cause a destruction of what was an otherwise difficult, but feasible first step toward solution, in the Greek case.

And so, again. This was not an accident, though it would appear to have been an accident. In other words, it would appear that the British Queen *had not* intervened in the way she did with two interventions in Germany , to organize this attack on the Greeks, but the situation was there potentially. But then, what hap-

Barack Obama toasts the Queen in London, May 25, 2011.

White House/Pete Souza

pened is, the British Empire again put a heavy hand on Europe, on Germany in particular, and a faction in Germany sold out to the British Empire! And sacrificed the Greeks in the process.

Now, that leads to conclusions: because what was done to the Greeks, is going to have a response. It doesn't mean that the Greeks are going to do it. It means that the logic of the situation is going to impel the situation in Europe to change course from what it would have been, if the Greeks had not been kicked around the way they were this past week.

So we're now in a new situation. The question is, what are the parties that were concerned, were dealing with the effects of this scheme, what are they doing to do, in terms of reaction? And if you look at the history of warfare, modern warfare in particular, but warfare in general, that is major warfare, or very serious warfare, we're in that kind of situation. We have not begun, *yet*, to experience the kind of operation which threatens us at this moment, as a result of what the Queen of England did in Germany against the Greeks. So it's not just a Greek issue: It's the consequences of what was done to the Greeks which is going to set off a chain-reaction effect, which has various routes to take. So now you're on the hot seat! But you don't know which end, to get your rear end off!

Q: Mostly what I do in my political activism is I write, because it's hard for me to express myself. In 1991, a conspiracy began and since 1991, the U.S.A. military has increased every single solitary year. April 15th—and I'm against the military and the prison industrial complex—on April 15th, 2013 that was a Patriots Day and a Tax Day, and on that day in the morning, I heard that War Resisters League was going to meet on 42nd St. in Times Square, and being an activist, I wrote to four different public schools about the military and the economic crisis; and by 12 o'clock when I got to Times Square, the Boston Marathon bombings had already happened. And I believe that was related to the Tea Party and the FBI.

But anyhow, during that time period, Rahm Emanuel came to Boston and took down the entire city. And during the time period, of immediate crisis, Obama was sending military—he was offering millions of dollars of military to Israel, Saudi Arabia, and United Arab Emirates; and at present they want to execute the boy who was a scapegoat.

I don't know what my question is, but it just really is very disturbing to me, a lot of the things our country is doing, so could you respond in any way? Thank you.

What is Actual History

LaRouche: Look, what happened? We had a reaction in the Senate, provoked by one of the senators; so we have four Senators who made a policy decision and the policy decision is still rolling around; it's still there. The question is, what is the activation, the next step which that implies? What *is* the next step? And what will we do about it? Then you have to anticipate, what's going to be the reaction? If you make that step, what's the reaction?

What's involved here. Look, Wall Street, as we know it, like the British Empire and like most of the trans-Atlantic community,—where most of the nations in that particular spectrum, as distinct from the trans-Pacific section which is completely different; but they all will come together with one big collision, if this thing goes in a certain direction. But right now, it's the question of the British role, in shaping the policy of the United States and the effects of this on the question of the trans-Atlantic/North Atlantic area in general. So that's what the issue is.

So the point is, how do we play this? See, it's not

like throwing balls, rolling balls around or something, and letting them hit each other; *this is not what happens in history*. What happens in history, is that mankind, either by negligence or by determination, changes the course of history. In other words, the whole history of mankind, is the history of mankind's changing of the course of history. And they can have *non*-participation, which is also an effect. What you don't do, is an action. That's the nature of mankind. I mean, aren't you alive? Don't you do things, don't you move or don't you

---

It's not like throwing balls, rolling balls around or something and letting them hit each other; this is not what happens in history. What happens in history, is that mankind, either by negligence or by determination, changes the course of history. In other words, the whole history of mankind, is the history of mankind's changing of the course of history.

---

decide not to move, as a human being when these matters come up?

Now this applies to you, personally. It applies to the little things you do or don't do in life; they're important; the education you got, or didn't get; the opportunity you got or didn't get;—all these things are factors. And the process of history is always *very active*, and therefore, you either act, or you don't act. And this applies to a large, broad part of the population of the planet. One area or another area reacts or the other one doesn't, or so forth. But the *interaction*, is constant! There is no such thing as a fixed system, which would be the idea that "it happened here, because he did this and she did that," and so forth. That is nonsense!

As you saw in the case of what happened to Hillary most recently: What was that? That was a very significant development, in the course of history, now. Hillary will never be the same, as she was up to the moment that she goofed. Then this caused an explosion. People in the area, a significant number of them, press and so forth, suddenly had to add a new factor to their policy, that Hillary was not the obvious Democratic Presidential candidate, *no longer* the obvious! She was the fake! She was the fool! She was a person you couldn't trust, the guy who was a swindler.

Then people reacted! The people who reacted, reacted in their way. The course of history was changed: History, in its essential nature, always moves. And the idea is that you have to be aware of the situation in which you're operating; not merely what happened yesterday, but what you did yesterday, is going to do for the next coming period of history. And that's what we have to do.

So the idea of trying to get neat formulas, like drawing on paper and so forth, that's nonsense. History is always that. And the most important thing in history, is discoveries of principle; discoveries of principles which mankind in general had never known before, or a large part of the population had never known before. Or, they have *failed*, to recognize what should have been recognized before!

There's no such thing as a simple, mechanistic way of measuring the course of history. And you look at the history of military warfare, major military warfare, in the course of the Nineteenth Century, the Twentieth Century and so forth,—very much that. But the problem is, that the practical person, so-called, the individual person, tends to be stupid, on this issue. They think that they are going to intervene in history; well, people do intervene in history. They can do that, yes. It's a good thing to do, if you do it the right way. But the point is *mankind is always moving*. Mankind is never at a standstill until it's dead, and even the death of a person has an active effect on the process, the political process as a whole.

So all these simple questions, simple answers, simple questions,— forget it! The question is to rise to an active understanding of what you feel is happening around you right now. And its effects on... you have competent leaders; well, if you don't have competent leaders, that's a bad thing! If you have good ones, you're lucky.

But always, things like scientific discoveries, you know, competent scientific discoveries, are really the thing that makes mankind live. And therefore, you have to be one of the active people in society, who's making things happen, which are in the effect of either new discoveries, or old discoveries which need to be moved. [applause]

Glass-Steagall and Impeachment

Q: Hello Brother LaRouche. I'm from Brooklyn. We all know how important Glass-Steagall is, and it needs to be reinstated to stop Wall Street and the global bankers. My question is, how will Glass-Steagall enhance the impeachment of Obama?

LaRouche: OK! Well, first of all, you can't make a fixed object, even a good one or a bad one; you have to move yourself. The answer's going to be in what we do, or what some people do to change the situation, or don't change the situation. And sometimes not changing the situation can seem to be the worst thing you can do, but sometimes there are cases you will regret, that you ever did it!

So this is really what's going on. Mankind has to function in society as an active force in society. Like you have to care about people. You have to care about them. And if you know something's going to happen that's bad to them, you should intervene in some way to try to make this bad thing go away.

Mankind has to be always on the alert. And mankind doesn't always know everything, but most of us know something, something we know from experience in particular. And we have to think about that, and think about the opposite choice. We have to think about them, we have to make decisions.

Now generally what we want to do, is increase the productive powers of labor. Now, that's not just simply work, that's the way you live. In other words, you want to fight disease, all the time. You want to defend people against disease, all the time. You want to improve your ability to conquer disease, all the time.

You want to create new discoveries; for example, now we're making great new discoveries. One of the greatest discoveries we're making right now, is the study of the Galactic System. In other words, mankind heretofore, had believed, that what happens in the Solar System in terms of action is the nature of man's condition in life. But then, we come up with new discoveries, and we discover that the Galactic System, is actually the dominant feature determining the fate of the human species. That is, in that context.

So therefore, if you don't do something about that, if you don't recognize that, all your dreams and all your fantasies don't mean too much. Because you're not in reality. And the characteristic of mankind is—you know, animals die, that is, species of animals die. But just think about what the history of humanity is. How

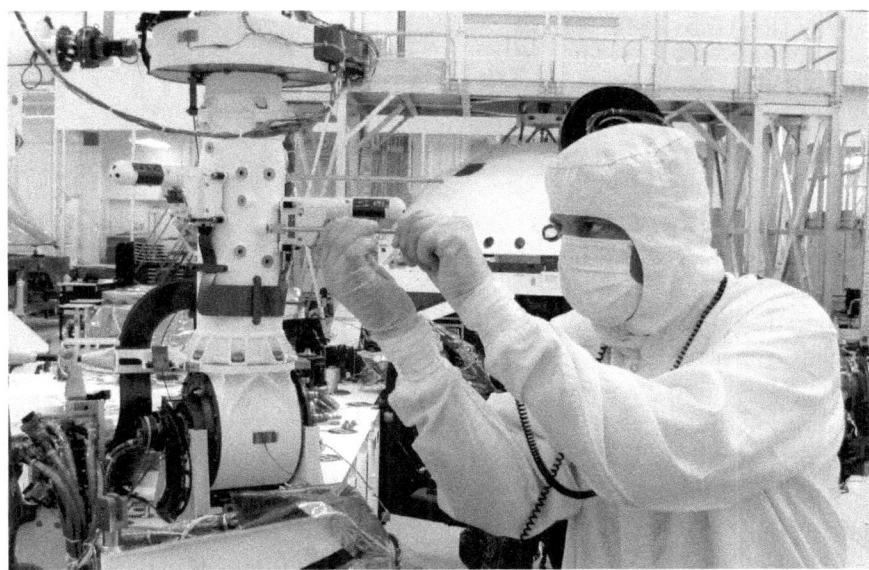

NASA/JPL-Caltech

A NASA scientist calibrates two finger-like mini-booms on the Mars rover Curiosity, in preparation for its voyage. It landed on Mars in August 2012.

many kinds of animals have died out, during the time that mankind was also occupying space on this planet? What's the difference? Mankind has the creative powers. *Animals do not have those creative powers.* Only human beings.

And the question is, to what degree do human beings develop improvements in their understanding and practice of reaching progress? For example, right now, what's the great danger now? The great danger now, happens when the British Empire took charge of the Pope. At that point, the British Empire, by pressing the Pope, began to push a process of cutting the population of the planet, cutting it from about seven billion living people, to less than one billion living people: That's the policy of the British Empire now! The British Empire is the actual director, the mother and director of Obama right now; the Bushes also tried to be this kind of thing as Presidents and similar types.

So the problem here, is we have to understand the responsibility of mankind to be mankind, which means to always move toward progress, to better health-care systems, for example. Not just health-care systems, but the protection of the life of human beings. Those are the opportunities, to survive and rise to a higher level of achievement, for the cause of mankind in general.

This is the only thing you can count on. There are no fixed advantages in history. Especially in terms of human history. Human beings are a unique species. We have no evidence of any other such species, that is living species as we know of living species. The human species is the only one that's properly in permanency. And the progress of mankind is like the discovery of the United States, the creation of the United States, in opposition to the British Empire, which was a force of Satanic evil in itself. The failures in Europe, compared to what the United States Constitution and its organization under Alexander Hamilton's leadership and guidance on many of these issues, created the United States as a superior culture. And the problems we have mostly in the United States today, is people forgot the name of the person who made the greatest specific barrage of changes in policy which made the successful establishment of the United States possible.

EIRNS/Robert Wesser

LaRouche PAC activists rally to revive Hamilton's program at Federal Hall, Manhattan, on July 16, 2015.

Conspiracy Theories

Q: The people, or the masses: how do you go about breaking them up, informing them, or you know, because it's hard to get them to say that it's not a conspiracy theory and turn their brain off?

LaRouche: Well, I think a conspiracy theory in this case is very useful. As a matter of fact, it's mandatory. Without a conspiracy theory, you wouldn't have the United States, for example.

Q: It would be good, if they didn't just turn off. It's like, if you know, if you say "conspiracy theory," that's it, it's just a different—they don't—

LaRouche: Exactly! That's what I do! This is my profession!

Q: I know, I know. I understand! But they don't....

LaRouche: Don't let people do that, don't let them! Stop it! Let them come alive, and find out what the news is that they should be getting, on which they should operate. It's the question of the person who rises to a more fully developed dignity, in terms of their self-estima-

tion of what their responsibility is in society. Call them the "creative leaders," the people who care! The people who come up with the solutions, where other people see no solution. Wars and so forth, they all come in that same category, you know.

The point is, you've got to mobilize the people, and you have to mobilize them by inspiring them to recognize what they have in themselves. Look, let's take a case, a good case: Let's take the case of the Civil War in the United States. Was the Civil War in the United States necessary? What was wrong with the Civil War success? It wasn't permanent enough. It's that simple!

So therefore, the actions that should have occurred were suppressed. We had a couple of Presidents, you know, general officers, two of them, and they were really good; and we had some later, very good. We won our wars, where we won ones, actually by having good leaders in the military leadership and in the political leadership. But it was always creative! Coming up with new discoveries.

What's happened to us? We don't make discoveries any more, we don't *want* discoveries to be made any more! We're cutting this out. We don't have nuclear power to use any more, generally; we don't! Do you know what that *does* as a threat to the existence of the human species, to lack the benefit of thermonuclear power and its improvement? Now we can control it; mankind knows how do control this. We have the technology! But they don't want to do it, they say well, they want to go back to the "green."

What's killing us? *The green!* The green philosophy is the greatest source of murder, of citizens of the United States today! It's a mass killing!

So my point here, is you cannot come up with pre-fixed, fixed kinds of things. Mankind is an active species. It's a species that is destined, by its nature, to rise to higher levels of achievement of the human species. Look, mankind is now on the road, like what happened in the Pluto case, just recently in experiment; not completed. But it shows that everything we thought about the Solar System was greatly underestimated, and that the Solar System is a much more interesting phenomenon than we had ever thought before.

Similarly, we are going into a position where we are looking for water. Well, how can you get adequate water supplies, under all kinds of conditions? Well the only way you can do that, essentially, comes down to, we have the largest source of water available to mankind which happens to be located in the Galaxy. That is a phenomenon which seems to us far removed from anything on Earth. But precisely that thing which seems so far removed, is actually greatly close at hand and decisive!

So the problem is, we don't *think* properly! We call it being *practical*, and what kills people is the foolish idea that they should be practical. [applause]

LaRouche, Putin and Clinton

Diane Sare: This is a question from someone who's listening and reflects their own intimidation by this extreme wartime propaganda that we're experiencing around Russia. The person writes that a few months ago, the Senate passed a law to control the news media about Russia, and that there has been spectacular anti-Russian propaganda, in the radio, television; and the person says, "they must have paid them a lot to get them to do this." So it's a very aggressive campaign against Putin in the United States, and they would like your comments on dealing with this.

LaRouche: Well, I happen to be something of an expert on Putin, and also on Russia from that whole period of my life, where I first visited Russia. And I went there a number of times, and I have a pretty good

NASA/Johns Hopkins University Applied Physics Laboratory/Southwest Research Institute

This photograph, taken July 13 just hours before the New Horizon spacecraft's closest encounter approach to Pluto, shows extremely varied and complex surface features and geology that were unexpected. Upon closer examination, the heart-shaped feature in the lower center, measuring about 1,000 miles across, was found to be an ice-covered surface, divided into segments of irregular shapes. It borders a dark region of ice mountains, rising as high as 11,000 feet. It will take more than a year to acquire all of the data New Horizons has collected during the first investigation of the largest outer Solar System icy body.

knowledge of it.

I didn't actually know Putin directly, when I first knew of him, but I did come to know of him, when he took up a leading role in the Russian organization at that time.

But before that, with the breakdown of the Soviet Union or the destruction of the Soviet Union as such, it wasn't working any more; and so in that period, and up to the time that Putin became obvious to me—that is, I knew of him before, but not in the terms as the leadership of Russia. But in his appearance as a leader of Russia, I got to know him at a distance, but in fact, because I had good sources, I knew what the things were, and I actually did some studies on him.

But what's happened is, that Russia has gone through a number of wrestling matches of various kinds, with itself, its own membership, its own disintegration in part, with the odd deal and problem.

And when I worked with, in a sense, but in a funny

way, though, with Bill Clinton, with Bill Clinton before he got the thing thrown at him by the British Monarchy; it was the British Monarchy that really ruined Bill Clinton's life, and that happened at a period where Bill had made a delayed move on behalf of what I had recommended to him, that we do, that we do on the basis of what I'd received in Russia from the experts in the Russian government at that time, and they asked for my opinion on what we could do to deal with the economic crisis which Russia was going through then.

So I came up with a proposal, in reply to the request to me from the central Russian leadership at that time. Of course, I was in touch with Bill, and Bill said, in his own way—and he had his own way—, I'm not going to do it now. What he meant was he was going to wait until his re-election for a next term as President. He actually adopted the policy which I had recommended be adopted on behalf of the Russians. But it came a little bit too late; it was a crisis.

And then the Queen of England—and she was the one who did it—intervened to set up a trap to discredit Bill Clinton. Unfortunately, his wife never really understood that. It was just beyond her comprehension. She's not a bad person, but she has stubborn convictions, which even Bill can't cut through, and was making big mistakes. The last time I met Bill, I met him at a point Bill had left office, at the conclusion of his second term; and I met Bill and Hillary, encountered them when the reception for Bill of coming out of his position as President occurred. And she had no understanding of what this was all about. Really! She was just confused. "I don't understand. I don't understand." Bill understood very well. But Bill has made some mistakes since that time, because he's been through the mill, and he tried to survive by adapting to the mill. Therefore, he made some very serious mistakes; but under great pressure, including from her, and so forth.

So that's the way things work sometimes. The problem is, you always have to recognize that these kinds of problems, these opportunities and problems, alike, are things which lie in the future, and you can't know them unless you *know* the future, or at least know a very significant part of it; as I do, when I made my forecast in response to the Russian leadership, at that point, where I had transmitted my recommendation for Russia's

CSPAN

Hillary Clinton at The New School in New York City on July 13, 2015— before the surprise struck.

physical economic recovery to Bill. Bill had got a message to me: we're going to do it, but we're not going to do it right away. And I was not happy about that.

But, then in the opening of the second term as President, he moved immediately on that policy. *Then*, immediately, the British Queen, the present British Queen, the old biddy, personally intervened, and she used her instruments in Britain as the convoy, the channel, to take over the control of the leadership of the Republican Party. Also, Bill's Vice President, who is a bit of a political whore, and Bill knew that by that time, so this was the problem that set him up. So he was set up.

This whole thing was really a booby-trap. The story about Bill and sex and so forth at that point, is not exactly the story. The story is it was a set-up, the set-up he was trapped into, and he was set up by his Vice President. His own Vice President set him up on that one. And that's the way history goes often. [Laughs] You have to take into account real history, not the, shall we say, the manufactured version.

Speed: [laughs] There are many baffled faces in the audience. But we have more questions. I also have one, but go ahead.

After Glass-Steagall

Q: Hi Lyndon, It's Daniel again. I felt as if I wasn't totally prepared, when I came up the first time, because, I was thinking—here we have what you're saying on the Queen. If people haven't seen it, there are wonderful pictures of the Queen as a young child saluting in the Nazi salute that came out in the British tabloids today. So if anyone has any doubts at all about what Lyn is saying, these people are much worse than Hitler.

And so, I'm thinking about, after what we did on Monday with Hillary, I was able to talk to people all over the country about what's changing. And it's been changing every moment. There's a rapid consolidation of the Glass-Steagall movement within the Democratic Party. And it's clear we're in a completely new terrain on that front.

But when I was talking to many people who are contacts and friends of ours, and supporters, from various parts of the country, it occurs to me to think again about your Four Laws statement that you produced just over a year ago, and I'm asking, Glass-Steagall flushes the evil, it separates the fraud from the reality, and therefore it's entirely and utterly necessary, and in that sense it's exactly the same thing as bringing down Obama, and so the victory on this is so absolutely needed.

And it's not nearly enough. And what we have to do is instruct the American people, in particular the leadership of the American people, about what it means to create real value, and how Alexander Hamilton returning to life, or, that is to say, continuing to live ever greater through us, is going to be needed to actually deal with the immediate consequences of restoring Glass-Steagall. We're going to have to extend long-term credit to build up the nation. We're going to have to achieve the increase of the physical productivity of our nation rapidly and protect our people who are going to be in a very vulnerable state, as they're watching this great change around them. I think they'll be very optimistic, but they'll be vulnerable at the same time.

So what occurred to me, having talked to these many people all over, is to ask myself how am I going to give them a sense of what real human economy is? If Glass-Steagall flushes the toilet, what comes next?

LaRouche: (Laughs) That's not a nice image. I think we should find a better image for that. The problem is the question ... the existence of the human species depends upon the equivalent of scientific progress. We can say that's the *category*; it's not just scientific progress per se; it's the category. It's the ability of the human species to rise from the evil, the Satanic evil, of Zeus, for example, who was the ancient Greek image of Satan, literally Satan. As opposed to what Nicholas of Cusa did in resuscitating civilization, together with other people who were part of the same pattern that he was leading, in leading to do things in Cusa's own work, which is really revolutionary.

At that point Greece, for example, when Cusa first reached, and examined Greece, went to the temple areas, which had excellent records, but the Greeks weren't practicing it any more. And so Cusa, Nicholas of Cusa, then turned around and said, "We've got to bring this back." So his understanding of Christianity, this principle, was based on the fact that here was something that Cusa brought back and worked on and developed, that corresponded to the reality of a Christian doctrine, the reality of the law which should govern mankind, but mankind's progress.

The key thing here is always mankind must progress. Mankind must progress by improving the powers of mankind as a species, to do things that no person has ever done before. And that's the principle: what has never been done before is what must be done next, including fixing up some errors that had been run up in the process in the meantime. But that's what mankind depends upon.

And what's happening now in the Green policy, what has now become popularized in the trans-Atlantic region: the Green policy is actually Satanic, explicitly, in its own essence. In other words, the British Queen is a Satanic force, by that standard, because mankind's ability to exist depends upon mankind's achievement of what are measures which are tantamount, in effect, to new physical principles or higher physical principles. That is the sense that mankind will and should be able to progress scientifically in order to get more control over the water that mankind needs on Earth, through control of mechanisms through the Galaxy, which is a very far distance from the surface of Earth as such. Mankind's scientific progress, the development of nuclear power, and higher orders of power which were generated in terms of echo of the successful nuclear power,—that is the standard on which the continued existence of the human species depends.

Progress! Green is the devil. Devilish poison. Green is bad; it's rotten; it's evil. It destroys the minds of people. It destroys their ability, makes them beasts, because they become like beasts. They become like slaves. Slaves weren't allowed to have progress. That didn't do them any good, did it?

And you saw what happened with the Civil War—people who had been slaves for a long period of time, suddenly emerged as talented geniuses, and things like that. They got freed. And since they lived in an environment, even as slaves, where in some parts of society, they had access to knowledge that there was a way of living which they were denied, which they knew about, they were cheated. Brick-layers, for example. African slaves, came into the Southern states, and some of them functioned as bricklayers, and the bricklayer was a step up. And the very fact that they get this kind of thing, some degree of skill, they recognized, why can't we use our skills and our brainpower as skills, to do what mankind should do? And so the problem in mankind's history is when people say, "Let's be practical." And you should say, "Well, you mean you want to die?"

Speed: I'm exercising the prerogative of the moderator. I can't resist; this is too good. The issue that you are bring-

After the Civil War, "people who had been slaves for a long period of time, suddenly emerged as talented geniuses..." Here, leading botanist George Washington Carver (c. 1861-1943), born into slavery.

ing up here, and which has been central to my discussion with you my entire life, which people call race, all the time, and they talk about Obama in this same regard, and so forth: what's the truth? This business with the Queen of England, and the videotape where she's seven years old and she's giving the Nazi salute together with her uncle Edward VIII. He's teaching her that, yes, but, that is her outlook from the age of 7, and the thing that we're talking about now, with the reduction of the population from seven billion to one billion, is a completely conscious and deliberate outlook.

Now, this makes me think of the following. Lyn, as you know, in the Catholic Church, the issue of reason at the age of seven, is the issue of the sacrament of Confirmation. In other words, it's said, when you're a child, you are a child until the age of seven. That age, reason takes over, and you receive what's called the sacrament

of Confirmation, which is sometimes given at the age of eight, and in this sacrament, there's a very specific thing that happens: you're given a name, you take a name, and you have a confirmation name. So for example, in my case, my confirmation name chosen by me was Jerome, after St. Jerome. And what they do, when you have Confirmation is, you're slapped on the cheek, which is supposed to symbolize your being oppressed, but defending the faith. So you take that slap on the cheek, okay, as an expression of your conscious defense of it.

Now, the reason I'm pointing this up is, because this woman, the Queen of England, and everything she represents, is not only Satanic, it's consciously that from the age of seven. Obama, who works with her, is consciously, deliberately, and fully a Satanic figure in every sense that Lyn has ever said.

Now this is often been, and everyone here knows it, it's thrown in people's faces, that Lyn is being a racist because he's attacking Obama, ostensibly because Obama is black. The truth is, Obama, the Queen of England and these people, are willfully, they're racist: They're opposed to the human race. [applause]

I just want to take this up, because what you've been talking about here, in the last period, is not just a matter of race It's also the other side of what you keep saying, which is, if you intervene in history the right way, if you do it on behalf of the love of people, and against things like the green policy, these other things—*this* is the way that history is actually changed.

This is the same thing that's done with Lincoln. Lincoln is often referred to, and Grant as well, somehow they have differences, they vacillate—no such thing is the case. Without Lincoln, there was no end of slavery. There was a deliberate fight, but as Lyn just said, it was never concluded. King, Martin Luther King, and others attempted to do that.

But this thing that you keep hitting at about the choice of being human, and the idea that these people are pursuing a Satanic policy, and that what we're doing is the opposite of that—it's a Promethean approach, as opposed to a Zeusian approach—whenever you bring this up, this just gets me most excited; but I love it because it's so stark in terms of the truth that people can *make this choice*. It's in everybody's power to choose to be human, and it's in people's power to choose to *not* be. And there are people who have done that, you can't deny that. You can't act like that's a formal question or a political question: It's a moral question. I'm sorry, Lyn, but I had to say that....

Our Species Goes to School

Q: B— from New Jersey. Again, Daniel has pre-empted something. And Dennis brought this up again, also. I have seen the video—it's now been spread through the internet—of the Royal Family practicing their Hitler salute as Hitler was being brought to power in Germany. And again, here in the U.S. we had a similar circumstance with the Bush family, you know, with Prescott Bush and others.

On the other side of that, you had Franklin Roosevelt, who was taking that on completely, particularly through Glass-Steagall and other measures that would allow the U.S. to take that fight on. And again, it was his understanding of both his place in and also looking back to Hamilton, that allowed that to occur.

You've brought this up many times, that within, effectively, the bones of the American people, are the capability to overcome what we now face domestically and internationally, and you've also brought up the role of the Presidency, which can clearly be seen with the George Washington Administration, Lincoln, and particularly Roosevelt, and you've brought up the role of the Presidency *now*, in being able to take this on again. And I'd like you to give us your insight into that, the present development of a Presidency.

LaRouche: Well, I just made some reference to that general area, and you've spoken on this thing, adequately in general.

But to make a more specific point, is what I've said earlier, which you've emphasized: science, true science, physical science. We understand things that mankind is able to use, that mankind had always had available to mankind, but mankind began to learn how to use it. Each step in that process brings mankind to a higher level in the Solar System, and also in the Galaxy as such—as such.

And the problem is that mankind's progress, like a child going to school, that the human species must go through that kind of progress, a special kind of higher school. Where mankind through development, is able to make changes in the universe, or at least parts of the universe, important parts on Earth, in particular. And nearby Earth. And mankind's ability to master these

---

And the problem is that mankind's progress—like a child going to school—that the human species must go through that kind of progress, a special kind of higher school. Where mankind through development, is able to make changes in the universe, or at least parts of the universe, important parts on Earth in particular. And nearby Earth.

---

technologies, as we call them, is the precondition for the continued existence of the human species, of mankind. And therefore, everything we do should be under a schooling system.

Now we used to have an idea what a schooling system was in the United States and elsewhere. You would have people who would get promoted for their skills, for their apparent skills, those skills were encouraged. Sometimes the effort to encourage was successful, sometimes it was not. But the process was, in the net effect, in the course of mankind's development, there were people who *did*, like Einstein in the Twentieth Century, for example, who *did* make general revolutions in man's knowledge and practice, which are still resonating as new conceptions today.

So therefore the issue of life is not what you achieve, *per se*—it's what you contribute to the progress of mankind's powers to create. And that's the difference. Only mankind can do that.

Also, by derivative, that no man is free, unless mankind is actually progressing in the equivalent of scientific skills *and their application*. It's not only the discovery of physical principles, and related things, it's the discovery of how you *use* those discoveries themselves to create new instruments from those discoveries, which open the gates for mankind's rise to a higher level, not only *on* the surface of Earth, but now, beyond Earth. What we saw this little funny thing that happened in space nearby—not so nearby—which is still being puzzled-over by the specialists. And that effort is going to open up something new. We don't know what that is going to be; we have to wait 'til we get it. Once it's delivered to you, then you'll know what it is, maybe.

Q: Good afternoon, Mr. La-Rouche, I'm P— from Connecticut, and I have a quick question. When Glass-Steagall is reinstated, and the commercial and investment banks are separate, what would happen to the depositors' money, like investment banks and the stock market?

LaRouche: Okay, simple. The problem with what the stock market is doing is actually destroying the economy of the United States, including the welfare of even rich people. Because most of these guys who are involved in Wall Street speculation are already hopelessly dead. They just haven't been buried yet.

What happened is, to take a practical case— We had a meeting of the Senate. One Senator brought that meeting around in the form of an action. Three other Senators joined her. The program that's now there; it's stirred the mud, shall we say. And it will continue to do so, I think, so far. And there's a knowledge that Wall Street is hopelessly bankrupt, and that the wealth of Wall Street is worthless intrinsically. We're going to have to do without all that money that Wall Street claims to own. We're going to cancel it. Why are we going to cancel it? Because it's cancelling itself.

Wall Street is now broke, totally broke. Just like a parasite, sucking on whatever it can suck—it's not producing anything anymore. So what's needed—we cancel Wall Street. That means that all the money that's listed as Wall Street assets pretty much *vanishes*, permanently, will never come back again. Good.

And the people who were practicing on Wall Street are going to have to find a new career for themselves, because the old one isn't going to work anymore; it's over, it's already over. That's one of the real reasons.

The whole trans-Atlantic community, in terms of

The WPA (Works Progress Administration) was a "school," "a parking place to keep people alive economically, until we could get them employed in real skills." Here WPA workers pour concrete on a storage unit in Ogden, Utah, in 1936.

Wall Street and similar kinds of financial systems, is *bankrupt, hopelessly bankrupt. Nothing can be done to save it in that form.* And the answer is, we have a Presidency, a national system, a national Presidential system. And our system provides automatically—okay, as Franklin Roosevelt demonstrated, this stuff is worthless, Wall Street assets are worthless, they're a threat to humanity, they're a poison. Franklin Roosevelt made that clear. Did the people of the United States lose, relative to the decade of my birth, which was a farce in the economy, and then when I, later, 1932, suddenly I found around me—and I was still just a young squirt, ten years old—but we found a change was going on. The education was improving in many places. The operations were gradually improving.

We went through the WPA (Works Progress Administration), for example. That was just a school, this thing; but it was a parking place to keep people alive economically, until we could get them employed in real skills. Like our miracles, in our efforts in building up for World War II. We *lived* on World War II. We fought and died, in the course of World War II. Why? For the sake of humanity. And we have not lost that.

Since Franklin Roosevelt's death, almost the moment he died, the general social trend, and the social practice in the United States, has overall degenerated at an accelerating rate since Franklin Roosevelt died.

As a matter of fact, when I worked under the leadership of Ronald Reagan as President for a short period of time doing a crucial thing called the Strategic Defense Initiative, which was my particular assignment, we were making progress even then. But then when the President was shot, and took some time to recover, then the Bush factor began to be pushed. That is, the Bush family descended from Prescott Bush; who was Mr. Evil himself; he was an intelligent Satan, the other Bushes were dumb Satans. That's generally a fair way of putting it.

So, we've now gone into a period—since that time—that is, since the end of World War II, since the end of the life of Franklin Roosevelt, in the general direction of life throughout the United States and throughout much of the planet, especially the trans-Atlantic period, that has been a failure. And if you want to see what's going on out there; you just have to see that. And I've lived long enough, since 1922 when I was born, to know as an adult, an active adult, that thing. I was already an expert at that point in economic function, back in 1944. So, we've gone to Hell since then. You know that some things were still good, some things were still nice; there were some opportunities and so forth.

But look at it today. Look at it under the most recent Bush administration; that's horrible, it's monstrous, disgusting. But under Obama is far worse; it's Satanism itself in practice. And the British Queen runs the show, globally. Some parts of the planet have resisted; some parts of Asia, some parts of South America, a spot here and there into South Africa and Africa. But otherwise, the whole culture of mankind since particularly the end of 1944 until now, since I went into the business of becoming an official, things of that sort; it's been going down, down, down, down, down, with no net improvement. Not even sustaining what we had achieved earlier.

Look at it; just take the conditions, just take the short time. See, most people in the United States today don't know what the truth is about their own history, or their own family's history; because they live in a period where they, as children—four to five years of age, where they begin to understand something—they don't know the past. They only know the past as a future; you know, what they attribute to its future; they don't know it. They don't really know often what happens at their

age of 20 years of age, 21 years of age; and that's what happens.

Most of our young people, who are young people below their 30s, have very—on the average—are completely incompetent. They have no competency whatsoever; that is, the things they do, do not contribute to the welfare of humanity. As a matter of fact, the effect is, that each decade since that time, has been a decade of decadence as such for the population of the United States as a whole. We have a few fat cats who sit there, supervising the thing, but doing almost nothing to fix it. [applause]

Q: Hello Teacher, and Helga. This is Mr. U—and M—saying hello to you with our Christian. Would the new Presidency that you are organizing be based on the attributes of the Rushmore Four; Jefferson's Virginia Statute, Lincoln's Railroad, Washington's Hamiltonian bank, Roosevelt's Glass-Steagall?

LaRouche: Well, I think we know now, that we have to cancel the influence of Wall Street entirely; there's no room for Wall Street anymore, it has to be wiped off the books entirely. That means a cut, a very large cut, in what's called the circulating money. Why is it cut? Because it can't circulate anymore; it's like you got blood, but the blood doesn't move, so you're going to die of quiet blood. And that's the case here.

If we restore Glass-Steagall, that in itself will be an included feature, an essential feature on which the recovery of the economy of the United States and its conditions of life will depend. That's the issue. We can fix it, but we have to have the opportunity to fix it; and we have to have people around us who know how to fix it. But essentially, it really is not much different than the intention of the Franklin Roosevelt administration. The details are different in terms of technology, but the principle is the same.

Social Conditions in New York

Speed: We're going to take two more questions.

Q: That's H—from the Bronx. I just thought since we're centering this process in New York City, just thinking of the conditions of life in New York City, where because of things like the real estate market, it's getting difficult to exist in New York City. The oligarchy around the world with their little *pied-a-terres*, these little apartment buildings and 100-story things on 57th Street. And obviously, they don't even live in them. And some of us are somewhat sheltered because we have either public housing, or cheap condominiums, cheap co-ops; but we also have new regulations, like what you said, the green energy coming in to make things more expensive for us. And you have the high level of homelessness; some people can work but they can't pay the rents, or other people, they just need supervision and the services aren't there.

So, I just want to know if you have any reflections of what we have in New York City. And then, just on a different subject, in the drug industry, we have cures or near-cures for things like hepatitis B, hepatitis C, and they don't even seem to be used at the rate that's necessary; that's something else I wanted to bring up. We have drugs, and they're not even being used.

Classical music in New York's Central Park.

youtube

LaRouche: We got a general problem in this whole area. New York City is a good subject to focus on, because New York City is one of the most important surviving areas of culture actually in the United States. And it's amazing that the culture in New York City is maintained by the part of the population and a few others, scientific and so forth. Where what I know from reflections, and therefore from experience earlier and from reflections, is that actually there's been a progressive degeneration of the human aspect of New York City and its environment. You see, skyscrapers are sometimes very doubtful in their value. You're getting a lot of people doing things, and scattering things around and so forth, which don't do any good for the people of that nature.

So, what we need, of course, is a change in policy; which will have to be done in a very careful way, to recognize that there are certain things that are done in New York City which do follow a tradition of real progress, not fantasy progress, real progress. Entertainment, social processes.

For example, we used to have Classical musicians in New York City—young ones. There used to be, in the period going into World War II, you find them up at certain areas, where these students who were becoming musicians, becoming professional musicians, would be gathered. They wouldn't have much money, but they would go in known areas, centered on Central Park; and these areas, they would settle, they would go there, and they would find out cheap or free tickets into musical events.

And they were welcomed by limitations; in other words, were the seats available for them, were the gates open for them. If they're musicians, they would say, they're musicians, training, don't have much money; all right, let's bring them in. Because they're the people who are going to be the audiences and the performers of the drama and so forth which are going to occur in that same population. And I knew a lot of people like that, who were living like that; before the war, and after the war had begun. So, we do have things; we have certain scientific institutions which are extremely important. Some of our best educational institutions which are extremely important. The basic educational system of the New York system has to be maintained at its best level; but an up-to-date level as well.

So, these are the kinds of things which should be taken into account. Obviously, what we build up in New York is, we build up a heavy weight of skyscrapers and things, which is, and the same thing happened in Germany; in certain parts of Germany, the same thing. Absolutely crazy skyscraper business, with absolutely no reason to exist there; because it's all this Wall Street kind of thing, or things related to Wall Street kinds of things which are producing most of these things. When we have a couple of skyscrapers in Manhattan, when I first lived there, these were unique; you were really impressed by these few places. But then we come down today, and you think, where's all this junk coming from. Why are the skyscrapers so high? It takes a week to get up and down the elevators; I don't know, it's silly.

But the point is, we do need a general social reform of the United States and other nations—like European nations—we do need a social process which makes sense for mankind, and the people who have to live in this process; we have to make it practical for them in a sense. How much are they going to waste their time chasing around for this or that, or this or that? As opposed to how much times they can concentrate on developing their own mental powers, and make their inventions and so forth—their arts, creation.

A portrait of German conductor Wilhelm Furtwängler by Emil Orlik. Furtwängler said of his artistic approach:

"I am told that the more you rehearse, the better you play. This is wrong. We often try to reduce the unforeseen to a controllable level, to prevent a sudden impulse that escapes our ability to control, yet also responds to an obscure desire. Let's allow improvisation to have its place and play its role. I think that the true interpreter is the one who improvises We have mechanized the art of conducting to an awful degree, in the quest of perfection rather than of dream [...]

"Some of Michelangelo's sculptures are perfect, others are just outlined and the latter ones move me more than the first perfect ones because here I find the essence of desire, of the wakening dream. That's what really moves me: fixing without freezing in cement, allowing chance its opportunity."

Freedom Through Beauty

Q: Hi, Lyn. It's D—. I wanted to bring up that right before we saw you, we had a beautiful demonstration from Jessica, on how to breathe when you're singing. And some people were stunned by that. Diane then picked up the ball there, and she had people singing solfège. And we actually did solfège for the very beginning of Schubert's Ninth Symphony; and we did it, one section was the oboes, another did the horns, and another section did the violins. This was beautiful! And but I heard some people say, "Well, what does this have to do with politics?" And it made me think of Friedrich Schiller, who said that the only path to true political freedom is through beauty. And I wanted you to comment on this idea, of why we need beauty. I think what Daniel did on Monday with Hillary Clinton, that to me was beautiful. [laughter] But I'd like you to respond.

LaRouche: Well, the question is, how to we develop the minds of our citizens? How do we develop the minds in terms of these kinds of technologies that we use for those purposes? How do we organize as a society so that the creative powers of the individual human beings are brought into a more efficient relationship to themselves? I mean, like impossible journeys, impossible work which is not relevant to the function at all—not relevant to man's function. We want things that will work. We want educational institutions, we want medical care, health care; we want these things which go with a social process. And you put into it, after you've defined the social process, now you put in some of the gimmicks in there, which have to go to make the social process work and prosper, and develop. And that's what you essentially need.

You also need some good entertainment; but it has to be healthy entertainment. It has to be things that make people happy. When people get sick, they do sick things and so forth. But things that really important; inspire people! Inspire them to discover in themselves a desire to do something which they look at and say, "I'm glad I did that." And that's—sometimes people educate themselves. And that's all part of the process; you want that kind of process. Even gossiping among neighbors is often sometimes very useful, because they will bring up things with other neighbors, relatives and so forth; and it actually tends to be a creative process.

In New York City, there really used to be a potential for that; and this has become diminished because of the pure mechanics of the thing, of the process, which have ruined it to some degree. But New York City is actually one of the most advanced places culturally in the United States still today, even today.

Speed: OK, so we've come to the end again, Lyn.

And I'd like you to, in concluding remarks, if you would, evaluate. You've now done four of these things; and we're going to be doing a few more. Where do you evaluate we are, where do you want us to go in the next coming week?

LaRouche: What you want to do is, you want to teach this things as an educational process, which is funny in one sense, but not otherwise. The point is, if you bring people together to work together on sharing talents, sharing experience, and applying that efficiently to, so that mankind knows what they have to do … See, most people in most parts of the United States, don't know why they're living; they really don't. They have entertainment. Look at our young people, you know, 20-25 years of age or so, or even 30; how much do they know? How much do intelligence do they really represent? What do they do? What does it do for mankind? What, isn't it like a drug addiction, habit? Isn't most of it of that nature? Isn't it the popular opinion, the popular game that you play, and dump the next season?

No, the problem is, we don't have an orientation for the self-education, and education in general, of our people. We don't have a science-driver perspective; which was always the thing that made us successful when we were making ourselves successful. We have to go back to the same thing; we have to go back to those principles. Rediscover them! Become human again, really human.

That's what the problem is. And you can't explain all this in one breath, or even a few breaths. You have to create a community within the community. Where you create a community; you have a community, but you have within the community, you have another community which is emerging. That other community, which may temporarily be smaller, is nonetheless the source of inspiration, cultural inspiration, for the development and enriching of the whole population. And New York City can become that, readily again; it just takes a little stun and a little leverage to make it happen. [applause]

Speed: So, Lyn, I want to thank you on behalf of everybody here for what you've done today. I think you've really moved people to think about themselves in a completely different way. They may be shocked by it, but I think they're probably going to accept your challenge to act in a human fashion. Thank you again for everybody here. [applause]

A Turn of the Key In the Presidential Campaign

by Daniel Burke

July 20—When you hear your fellow human being announce imperiously, "Our fate is sealed," how do you respond? Do you sink back, allowing the statement to hang in the air, this blasphemous notion that the sublime creative force of human society has finally been explained away? Or do you rise to the standard of basic decency, to defend your species?

And once you've risen, what is required of an individual who seeks to represent the human species in the effort to defeat a Zeusian "fate?" What Promethean quality can deliver us across the unbridgeable chasm between this era and the next?

The morning of Monday, July 13, 2015, I sat with my LaRouche PAC colleague Judy Clark in a darkened auditorium in New York City. Hillary Clinton, known at the beginning of that speech as the "inevitable" winner of the Democratic nomination for United States President, had gathered the international press and a small group of students at The New School in Manhattan's Greenwich Village in order to present her intended economic policy to the nation for the first time. Several hundred people sat together listening to Senator Clinton, but I believe that none were more anxious than Judy and I. We hoped that Senator Clinton would have the insight and courage to address the most critical political process underway in the United States: the advancement of Glass-Steagall in the United States Senate, reintroduced as a bill on Tuesday, July 7th by Senators Elizabeth Warren, John McCain, Angus King, and Maria Cantwell.

Like many others in the audience, I knew the importance of the timing of the Warren bill, S. 1709, the existence of which was announced in the midst of the horrific collapse of the European financial system made evident by the murderous attacks on Greece by the craven team of Merkel and Schäuble and their current mistress, the British Queen. Unlike the other

LPAC/Michelle Fuchs

Daniel Burke, shown here, organizing in New York City in April 2015.

audience members, however, I had been present at a LaRouche PAC Town Hall in Manhattan on Saturday, July 11th, and I had heard Lyndon LaRouche say to his movement, in response to the actions of the four Senators:

> "The time has come to win, not to complain, but to win: The chance is now. We have to make it now."

Hillary Clinton did not speak the words, "Glass-Steagall," in her speech that morning, so I did. I rose to my feet as her speech came to a close, and I simply asked her, "Senator Clinton, will you restore Glass-Steagall?" She refused to meet my eyes, and refused to make any comment in response, so I asked again several times, each time with greater volume. The photographers in the center aisle began snapping photos, and security came to escort me out of the building.

Within moments, my question was reported around the world. I was quoted in interviews as a representative of Lyndon LaRouche's movement. That afternoon an economic adviser to Hillary Clinton, former Federal Reserve official Alan Blinder, was quoted in a Reuters news wire declaring, "You're not going to see Glass-Steagall," and claiming to have recently consulted with Hillary on exactly this question. Later, a second unnamed Clinton adviser contradicted Blinder, saying

"Nothing is off the table," but the damage had been done.

The presidential campaign, and thus history, had been changed. Clinton's credibility was erased. In refusing to respond to a basic principle of decency,—and in announcing her loyalties, through Blinder, to Obama and Wall Street,—she had doomed her current Presidential campaign.

Wednesday evening July 15 Senator Warren called on all Democrats to join her in restoring Glass-Steagall. Thursday, the same publication that had interviewed me on video the day of the intervention interviewed Democratic Presidential candidate Martin O'Malley, asking for his response to the question. O'Malley reiterated his stated position in favor of immediate restoration of Glass-Steagall. Friday, *Newsweek* published an article by Robert Reich, political economist and former U.S. Secretary of Labor under President Bill Clinton, decrying Hillary's actions. That same day, Obama's press secretary, Josh Earnest, was asked directly whether the President would support the move by Warren and her colleagues to restore Glass-Steagall. Of course he answered negatively, saying effectively, "We'll stick with Dodd-Frank."

Saturday morning, the *New York Times* announced that Senator Bernie Sanders had become the fifth co-sponsor of Senator Warren's 21st Century Glass-Steagall Act, and publicly challenged Clinton with the same question I had asked. They referred to a "heckler" in the audience of Clinton's New School speech. By Monday July 20, the City of London's *Financial Times* was forced to trot out Wall Street gremlin Barney Frank to attempt damage control.

Lyndon LaRouche's method of transforming history is so much more powerful than most of us are willing to admit to ourselves. No "fact" will shape the future of the Presidency of the United States. No statistic will walk in the door and end the British Empire. No war is won on the basis of a pre-defined schedule. The option to win a global victory of man, to graduate to our galactic destiny, lies within our grasp.

Every Day Counts In Today's Showdown To Save Civilization

That's why you need *EIR*'s **Daily Alert Service**, a strategic overview compiled with the input of Lyndon LaRouche, and delivered to your email 5 days a week.

Take the example of the ongoing debt showdown with Greece, which now threatens a blowout of the world financial system.

On June 18, *EIR*'s Daily Alert reported that the Greek parliamentary debt commission had issued a report declaring the bailout debt "odious" and "unpayable." On June 22, the Alert reported on an interview by former German Chancellor Helmut Schmidt, where he said the Greek debt was indeed unpayable.

Don't you think you should have known of these developments as they happened? Can you really afford to wait for the consequences?

THURSDAY, JUNE 18, 2015

EIR Daily Alert Service

EIR DAILY ALERT SERVICE P.O. BOX 17390, WASHINGTON, DC 20041-0390

- The Euro Is Bankrupt, Not the Drachma
- Hellenic Parliament Debt Truth Commission: All the Troika Debt Is Illegitimate
- Tsipras Is Ready To 'Say the Big No'
- Paris Conference: 'Rebuilding the World in the BRICS Era'
- Tsipras To Discuss Gas, BRICS Bank in Russia
- CIA IG Report: More Coverup of Saudi Role in 9/11
- Obama Tries End-Run Around Democratic Resistance to TPA
- Nemesis Strikes: Piggish Gabriel under Pressure To Step Down

EDITORIAL

The Euro Is Bankrupt, Not the Drachma

June 17 (EIRNS)—With the Greek Parliament's Debt Truth Commission having just found Greece's entire debt to the Troika to be "illegitimate and odious," *EIR*

Music Is Not Notes, It's the (In)tension

by Lyndon H. LaRouche, Jr.

The following was excerpted from a discussion between Mr. LaRouche and his associates on July 7, 2015.

Glass-Steagall is now on the agenda in the Senate. Now, when you look at the conditions of life in the United States and abroad, especially in Europe, but also elsewhere, Glass-Steagall is an igniting process. That is, it is not something you can close off on. Once people are told that Glass-Steagall is available, you're going to have a shock effect. It also will have an effect on music; it's going to have a shock effect on music. Once that thing is presented in the United States as Glass-Steagall, you're going to have a panic on Wall Street, which is a delightful thing to watch. That is crucial.

What's also crucial is a related thing, which is not often treated as being the same subject, but it is: the question of music. The principle of music is not script; it is not description, it is not popular music. Popular music is crap! Leave it to the pigs, but stand away from them because the rush will be great.

The point is, that mankind, inherently, has powers of existence which are the root of the musical composition of music, and this is historic; it goes back to the ancient Greeks and other things of that sort. Our situation is such that we have to understand this thing which is called music. The point is, where does this lie?

Where does all this thing about money and so forth

A musical competition depicted on a vase from Classical Greece.

and all these things—where does it lie in terms of human experience? It lies in something which is not a simple musical score. The greatest composers of music from before Bach, but especially since Bach up to Furtwängler—and Furtwängler was a key achiever after the entry into the Twentieth Century. The Twentieth Century was generally, in education generally, in so-called science generally, it was all a fake; absolutely a fake.

So what's the problem? What is music; and what is the meaning of music for mankind?

A State of the Human Mind

The fact is that the human mind is not a matter of notes. Though notes come into play, they are the shadows of reality, not the source of reality. The problem today is that we have so much unpopular music that people have lost their connection to music—in particular, for example, to Bach and the excitement caused by

Mozart, the higher excitement by Beethoven, Schumann as an inspirational element in the process of the evolution of Classical musical composition. And Brahms—Brahms's latest works were also great works, and they were each unique in their originality, and they were valid. They weren't just improvisations; they involved a matter of human principle, of the human mind's principle.

And Furtwängler, of course, is the exemplar of the post-World War II period. Even though he was born in an earlier period, his entire intention in music was located in Brahms and the other people who preceded him. He was the best expert, and is important in this in particular for us now, because we're looking for examples of this

Keeping the Classical tradition alive: Conductor Wilhelm Furtwängler (1886-1954).

principle which are more readily comprehended by people who are not the best trained in music. You want people who are not the best trained in music to be able to come up to a level which achieves something which they otherwise would not have accomplished. In other words, they have to struggle to find out what the discovery is, which is there. In the case of Furtwängler, Furtwängler did things which are most commonly referred to in terms of his treatment of the Schubert 9th Symphony.

All good proponents during the Twentieth Century proceeded with a reasonable attempt to continue the Classical musical composition principle. Now, this is not an animate object, it's not an experience as such; it's a principle of mankind, it's a principle of the human mind, because in all cases it reaches beyond what people can arrive at deductively. You have popular music, which is considered popular music; and you have also deductive music, which is destructive music—modern music, practical music. It's stupid, it's demoralizing; it's corrupting, it's polluting.

Yet the principle which underlies music is a principle of the human mind, which does not have a physical expression in and of itself. What Furtwängler did with the 9th Symphony of Schubert is a living example of what that distinction is. Most people who tried to perform the Schubert 9th Symphony got it wrong, because they were looking at it in simple terms of

notes and beats and so forth—the mechanical approach. If you listen very carefully to what Furtwängler did in that symphony, there's a silence in between the notes, and the silence is what defines the notes. That means that the person has to actually put their mind in a dimension which is not a so-called practical expression, not a simple physical principle. You can take all Classical music in general from particularly Bach on to the most recent time, and the note is never the basis *per se* for competent musical composition. Why?

Music is not music *per se*; music is a state of the human mind which finds its expression in new forms, insight into new forms, higher forms of insight into the nature of the human species, and in the progress of the human species. You cannot mechanically produce decent music; you have to have an inspiration. You have to envelop it internally, and let it envelop you. And when it envelops you, then you begin to understand yourself.

That's what you mean by the great performers. They were not rehearsing notes; they were creating an order in which the music flows, which is not the sound—it's the tension. The tension, not the sound. And anyone who performs competently in music, knows that. It's the tension which makes it. That's what Furtwängler did with the 9th Symphony of Schubert—the tension. If you listen very carefully to what he does with the opening of that symphony—don't listen for the note! Listen for the irony, the irony which lies within the domain of the set of notes. The notes as such have a special meaning, and the meaning is the difference between man and a monkey.

What Lies Between the Notes

The problem is that today we have lost sight of the meaning of humanity. We want a form of music which does not involve humanity, and that's the problem. When you say the literal note is the basis of music, that's idiocy! Anyone who really knows something about music, knows exactly what the implications are of that principle of composition. It's unique to human beings. It's unique to human beings who have an apprehension of what is the value of musical composition. Every competent musician wants to find that location, where the voice is placed and the tone is placed as such. It produces an effect which bestirs the soul of the individual person.

You have to uplift people, inspire them, which is the function of Classical music. But the sound is not the thing; it's the tension, not the sound. People can try to practice the thing in terms of the sound, and it doesn't work. It's the tension between the space of the sound; between the notes. It's a common expression: "Music lies between the notes." Now, what does it lie there for? It lies in the area of tension between the notes, and the role of the tension is what determines the quality of the music. It's the inspiration of a state of mind which is not based on sound, but is based on the tension which may be associated with sound.

It is that tension which makes the difference between an animal, a papier-mâché project, and a human being. It is the tension that lies between the cracks of the notes. And it is that tension, if you listen very carefully—a musician can do this, who's experienced. Look between the notes in Furtwängler's work, especially the opening of the first part [of Schubert's 9th Symphony], and look at how he paces the stress in the passage of the notes, between the passage of the notes. That's where the location of creative musical insight comes into obvious reality. The achievement of most of the greatest musicians, composers, is to rely on that principle. Mozart did; Bach already did. Beethoven did it. He was a genius at it. Others were there, important famous musical figures who were also poets. And the poem doesn't mean anything unless you understand where the stress is which lies principally behind and between the notes. That is the difference between music and a recording device; an idiot who can speak all day, but can't think.

An Out-of-Tune Culture

And therefore, we've come to a time where the idea of the identity of the human mind and the creative powers of the human mind are not arithmetic. Arithmetic is for stupid people, or dead people. The point is the inspiration of what man can mean, the progress of man; the indefinite progress of man's development; the ability of mankind to achieve things in space, including the Galaxy. Where's your galaxy score? It's an essential part which runs the universe! When did you last play your Galaxy? Well, we can play the Galaxy! It's by learning how to use the principle. It's not called music, but music is something which is an instrument of life. It's the instrument of life of a human being, whether they're a composer, or simply a child who's fascinated by a tuneful piece of music.

What we're dealing with now in the habits of the United States population in general, is that there is, out there, an existing, knowable principle which is associated most prominently with Classical musical composition. It also comes out in the form of ancient Greek poetry. The essential thing is that music is essentially a form of poetry, with a rather strict sense of when you're on tune, and when you're off tune for that purpose. Today, we have completely off-tune minds of people—that's the general characteristic. People today are not generally really human. They may be human physically, in physical behavior, but they have lost the connection to humanity. Humanity is not a procedure! It's not just a simple actor, it's not a machine. The human mind has no known duplication as a principle.

What we're dealing with is a degenerate culture; where classical poetry—including for example, ancient Greek poetry, which is a form of song; its characteristic is that of song, of music—has been lost. Wherever that has been lost, the tendency is to produce something like Zeus.

It is to call the spirit of the human individual—not the song as a mere fact, but the intention, the spirit of the motive. When people have lost that, you get Twentieth Century music, which is intrinsically garbage. Some people survived, despite being located in the Twentieth Century, but they didn't deserve such treatment.

Therefore, you have a problem now in music, or art, or everything of relevant human behavior: You have no contact with your own humanity, because you make yourself a machine. What we have lost is a connection to the medium of action by human minds, which actually define the human work.

Glass-Steagall is a good example of that. What's Glass-Steagall? It's creativity *per se!* So it's you, the human being inside you, that's in charge, not the pottery. And that's the danger of evil. We are induced more and more to surrender to the popularity of idiocy, of submitting to arbitrary values which are not values at all, and we lose the connection to humanity. And humanity is not a sound! Humanity is an experience of a tension, and all great composition and performance is based on that kind of intention, and tension. It's tension, as in intention, of a living human being which is what the principle is.

The question of teaching of people principles of science that mankind in general had never known before, that's music. That's the principle of music.

Being Human

The point is the activity based on a human principle, a purely human principle of discovery, not on a mechanical device, not on punching out notes on a piano, unless you can be clever and outwit the piano, and make it do things by the way you play it, which brings it to life. The music does not come from the piano; the piano comes from the music. And the people who are capable of doing something about that, are the people who have some insight into humanity. People who can't do that are just banging.

That's what the problem is. The issue is that the

EIRNS/Stuart Lewis

"Music is the instrument of life of a human being," LaRouche said. Here, young children performing a Classical concert in Leesburg, Virginia in August 1985.

creative powers inherent in mankind, as a potential, define the device which is not a sound, but is a stress, it's a tension; a tension which actually defines the activity of the human mind. What we've done in the United States recently, what popular music has done, is to destroy the humanity of the human individual. Most people who accept popular music are idiots, or worse.

All great music is born of human passion. And if you don't express passion, you ain't a musician! The whole thing is passion! It is to move people, to change the way they're thinking at that mood and time, as a constructive act. Constructive acts! Trying to uplift people to what they didn't know, trying to have them discover things which they thought they were incapable of doing. It is these tributes, which help us understand what humanity is.

In the United States now, under Wall Street influence and things like that, we have no human qualities insofar as we're part of that. Therefore Glass-Steagall is the human motivation among human individuals, in their purposeful actions for a useful effect for the sake of humanity. That's human. Everything else is a farce, and that is what is wrong with the United States right now. There is no human love in the process.

Max Planck and the Principle of Human Discovery in Music

by Caroline Hartmann

Great is the trust and confidence of mind wherever order becomes manifest. The cause of this is to be found in the deepest origins of geometry. Even if an order were to be effected by accident, the spirits would fly together into it; therein lies their delight, their life.

—Johannes Kepler, *Harmonia Mundi*, p. 5

July 11—In the midst of the period of discovery of mankind's greatest energy source to date, nuclear fission, the home of the physicist and musician Max Planck (1858-1947), who held the chair of Theoretical Physics at Friedrich Wilhelm University, was a constant meeting spot for music-loving scientists. Many fellow researchers, collaborators of Planck and students, such as Lise Meitner, Otto Hahn, Max von Laue, Arnold Sommerfeld, and Albert Einstein, were often guests. And music played, not by chance, an important role in this creative period of the waning Nineteenth Century!

Planck himself was a gifted pianist; he nearly became a musician instead of a physicist, having become closely associated with music while still a

Planck: Science cannot solve the ultimate mystery of nature.... Music and art are, to an extent, also attempts to solve, or at least express that mystery.

schoolboy. As a young student, he frequented many homes where the arts were cultivated; a lot of theater was performed, and Max Planck composed songs, small pieces, and even an operetta for such home performances. Gifted with perfect pitch, he sang soprano in boys' choirs, performing the great oratorios. He was second choirmaster in an academic glee club, and played the organ at church services in the student chapel. He was also conductor of the orchestra club, consisting of both professional artists and amateurs, while he worked to perfect his piano playing.

During his years of study in Berlin, he systematically pursued the piano, and seriously considered whether he ought to move entirely over to music. But he opted for physics, although he studied harmony and counterpoint when he was back in Munich again, with Professor Josef Rheinberger.

Einstein spoke once of Max Planck's "genuine artistic side" and his "artistic need that drove him to creative achievements." In fact, music played an important role in the circle of the Berlin physicist. Planck himself played the piano like a professional, and often, his friend and frequent guest was the great violinist Joseph

Joachim (1831-1907), who was director of the Academic College of Music at the time, and with whom he played Beethoven sonatas. Many other professional musicians admired him for his fine sensitivity to the intentions of the artist and the verve of his accompaniment. With the other physicists such as Einstein and Sommerfeld, but also with his son Erwin as 'cellist, trio or quartet evenings were often organized, where some of his students attended regularly. Reporting about one such music evening at Planck's home, Lise Meitner wrote to Otto Hahn in the Autumn of 1916:

"Yesterday I was with Planck. Two magnificent trios (Schubert and Beethoven) were played. Einstein played the violin, and volunteered, by the way, some of the most deliciously naïve and peculiar political and military views." (L. Meitner to O. Hahn, 16.11.1916, in: Sabine Ernst: *Lise Meitner Otto Hahn Letters from the Years 1912-1924*," Stuttgart, 1992, p. 64).

Otto Hahn, who discovered nuclear fission with Lise Meitner and Fritz Strassmann, had a powerful but untrained tenor voice himself. Through the music scene in Berlin he became acquainted with works of Classical music, and Planck even persuaded him to take singing lessons, as Walther Gerlach and Otto Hahn's grandson Dietrich write in their biography.

Whether it came to designing a difficult experiment, or to Planck's solution, a few years later in 1900, for the radiation law, Planck stuck with a problem, and was not satisfied with half-solutions as were other researchers. This trait was developed and strengthened by his preoccupation with the great works of Bach, Mozart, and Beethoven.

Whence the Power of Classical Music?

It is no coincidence that countless great scientists were also outstanding musicians, and Planck's testimony, as related by his wife's nephew Hans Hartmann in his biography, is of great importance: Planck made music not only for relaxation and recreation, but rather music represented a place in his life where his mind could develop freely! For him, music was not just a matter of feeling, but was also the world of his mind, his creative ideas.

Classical music thus played an important role in this pioneering time. It is not only a universal language that can express more than words; it reaches into the immediate and deepest experiences of the human soul, moving the soul in a creative way. How can one explain this power? Where does this power of music come

from? Ludwig van Beethoven once said that "Music is a higher revelation than all wisdom and philosophy."

What is Man? Why does he explore the laws of nature? Why does he dig up old layers of rock in order to explore ancient buildings and tombs? Why does he want to know the history of space, to discover the universe? Just what is this human soul? Plato has Socrates describe the soul in the *Phaedrus* as follows:

But first of all, let us view the affections and actions of the soul divine and human, and try to ascertain the truth about them. The beginning of our proof is as follows:

Every soul is immortal. For that which is ever moving is immortal; but that which moves something else or is moved by something else, when it ceases to move, ceases to live. Only that which moves itself, since it does not leave itself, never ceases to move, and this is also the source and beginning of motion for all other things which have motion. But the beginning is ungenerated. For everything that is generated must be generated from a beginning, but the beginning is not generated from anything; for if the beginning were generated from anything, it would not be generated from a beginning. And since it is ungenerated, it must be also indestructible; for if the beginning were destroyed, it would never be generated from anything nor anything else from it, since all things must be generated from a beginning. Thus that which moves itself must be the beginning of motion. And this can be neither destroyed nor generated, otherwise all the heavens and all generation must fall in ruin and stop and never again have any source of motion or origin. But since that which is moved by itself has been seen to be immortal, one who says that this self-motion is the essence and the very idea of the soul, will not be disgraced.

—Loeb translation, 245c-e

In this creative period in Berlin, Planck and the other physicists around him saw themselves not only as natural scientists but as artists as well. He once said about their calling:

It is not logic, but the creative imagination which ignites the first flash of insight in the spirit of the researcher who is advancing into dark regions ... and without imagination new fruitful ideas do not present themselves. For if, in the midst of the patient, often humble individual work which involves both mind and body, a thought strengthens and uplifts, that is what we physicists work for—not for today, not for momentary success, but, in a manner of speaking, for eternity.

Augustine: The Soul Does Not Want To Squander Itself

For millennia, men have been fascinated by the significant role of music. It bears upon the ancient paradox of what is Man, how body and mind are connected, because since music awakens feelings, but simultaneously works upon the soul and its conscious (and unconscious) thoughts, music is a means for bringing these two worlds together into reciprocal relationship!

Pythagoras was the first to systematically come to grips with this problem. In music one can observe a phenomenon whose basis nobody had previously questioned: There are only a very limited number of musical intervals that the human ear perceives as "beautiful." Pythagoras discerned that this is about proportions, that the human soul must reflect geometric proportions, and he was the first to seek out a cause underlying our capacity to perceive beauty. He made a discovery: the geometric "living" structure of aural space. Through these geometric proportions, he demonstrated why music is the universal language, and why it so profoundly touches the soul and the human creative spirit.

This knowledge made the further development of music in European culture possible for the first time. Pythagoras proved that with music, just as with geometry and astronomy, that human gift may be precisely expressed, which cannot be found by physical or physiological examination: the capacity for creative ideas.

More than 2,000 years after Pythagoras, the astronomer Johannes Kepler turned again to this paradox. On the basis of Pythagoras's discovery, he explored the connectedness of geometric knowledge with the harmonic lawfulness of the structure of the universe, and in the process made a further discovery about the true reasons for music's powerful effect:

No matter how old the form may be of human singing, which is composed of consonant and melodic intervals, the causes of the intervals

"St. Augustine in His Study," by Sandro Botticelli (1445-1510).

were hidden from humans, so that before Pythagoras not one person inquired about them. Now that they are being sought again after 2,000 years, I am, if I am not mistaken, the first to present them in the most accurate detail.

—Johannes Kepler
Harmonies of the World

Eight hundred years after Pythagoras, Aurelius Augustinus of Hippo, later known as St. Augustine (354-430 A.D.) from Thagaste in Numidia, a great admirer of Plato, grappled once again with this question in his writings. He is thus a lone voice against the cultural decay in the time of the collapsing Roman Empire. The musician and the listener must grow beyond the mere recording of musical impressions, and the superficial and sentimental devotion to the sonic, because, according to Augustine, "the soul does not want to squander itself" (Aurelius Augustinus, *De Musica*, Augustine German edition, 1962, p. 12).

The Greek scientist Pythagoras, depicted in a wooden sculpture by Jörg Syrlin, at the Cathedral at Ulm, Germany.

rThe beauty of music is grounded not only in the harmony of the individual tones. The real beauty has a much deeper cause. Nor is it a coincidence, that in the degenerative phases of history, music became increasingly superficial and primitive. For example, at the time of the Peloponnesian War, when the morality of Athens began to regress, and which is often called the "time of the comedies," comic actors appeared everywhere to malign and ridicule the ideas and teachings of Pythagoras, and to mock his remaining followers. Up until the final downfall of Athens, the cult of Dionysus spread its decadence, idleness, and self-indulgence, and the music was for pure pleasure, background music for cultic or military entertainments, or simply intoxicants for ecstasy (*ecstasy* = Greek word for "copping out"). Man was considered a creature of chance. In ancient Rome, St. Augustine had to contend with similar excesses, and in the Nineteenth Century Friedrich Nietzsche revived the cult of Dionysus again, in order to express his own hatred for humans as responsible for their ideas in history.

Today's spiritual degeneration was likewise set into motion for political reasons in 1947 by the Congress for Cultural Freedom, which primarily employed the primitivization of music. It was dubbed "popular music" or pop music, but it uses the same degenerate material as in all the earlier historical phases mentioned above: constant repetitions, unchanging rhythms, especially on pre-Pythagorean (e.g. pentatonic) scale-based tunes. Small wonder that they just "agitate" or "excite" people, whereas the soul and the mind do not respond. This music is not only itself dead, but it systematically kills the human soul and the spirit's yearning for something better! It is as if one were to bring a dead person, by electrical shocks, to make twitching motions, as Edgar Allan Poe describes in his short story "The Facts in the Case of M. Valdemar," but he is not brought back to life. The human mind, however, is alive, and is merely lulled by these primitive tricks into boredom, "switched to economy mode." The longer this continues, the more difficult it will be to reawaken the creative spirit!

It is not a "matter of taste," that what we term Classical music was developed by the Pythagoreans' discovery of the eight-step scale, of the various half-tone steps, and then further by Kepler, until finally after the Thirty Years War, we come to the work of music theorist, composer, and organist Andreas Werckmeister (1645-1706), consciously based on Kepler's work. Werckmeister was working for Dietrich Buxtehude when Johann Sebastian Bach met him while visiting Buxtehude. In his book *Musical Temperament* published 1686 in Frankfurt am Main and Leipzig, he refers to the well-tempering of organs, spinets, and all keyboard instruments, based explicitly on Pythagoras and Johannes Kepler and his idea of *harmonia mundi*.

Classical Music Is Not 'A Matter of Taste'

The development of Classical music is synonymous with exploring the workings of the creative powers of the human mind. It was based on the fact, discovered by Pythagoras, that the human mind perceives a certain number of selected proportions as consonant, which makes all other proportions dissonant. This creates the conditions where polyphonic composition must be based on certain principles! This is absolutely not arbitrary, but is determined by the human mind—or, you can say, the human soul itself! In his investigations into these proportions, Kepler comes to the conclusion that it is the authority of the soul, spiritual knowledge itself, which is linked to the beauty of these laws, and which ultimately recognizes them:

> The activities and movements of the body, where harmonious proportions are imitated, speak for the soul and spirit, in that they indicate the reason why consonances evoke delight. The

judgment of the ancients also does not contradict this. When they define the soul as a movement, as harmony, they did not speak utter nonsense, but rather they have not been properly understood, because often in difficult questions, a mystical sense is veiled under the cover of the word. The philosophy of Timaeus of Locri, where the soul is composed of harmonious proportions . . . , was refuted by Aristotle in the literal sense of the text. But I would say that not all that lies within those lines, is what the text alone says. Indeed, I do not think anyone will deny that the former author, at least in his fundamental thoughts, as I postulate it, holds that it is the soul and spirit of people, by whose judgment or instinct the hearing of the pleasant, i.e. consonant proportions, is distinct from the unpleasant or dissonant. He lays it out carefully on the consideration that the proportions are objects of the Understanding and can be grasped only by the mind, not by the senses, and that it is a function of the mind to distinguish the proportions, i.e. the form, from the thing proportioned, i.e. the matter.

—*Harmonies of the World*, Book III

Max Planck was aware of these investigations, as may be seen in his 1894 treatise "Natural Tuning in Modern Vocal Music" (Leipzig, Breitkopf & Härtel). Planck, Einstein, and his contemporaries were aware of this history of Classical music, the discovery of the creative power of the human mind. Therefore, their presentation of music was in many respects more alive with tension than that of the artists of today, despite the ever more perfect technique of the latter's performances! It is perhaps because of the awareness that the continually self-moving soul finds expression not only through sensory things, that it in fact represents the reason for what Man ought to do. As Gauss expressed it:

There is in this world a pleasure of the mind which satisfies itself in science, and a pleasure of the heart, which lies mainly in the fact that people ease one another's hardships, their lives' burdens. But if this is the task of the Supreme Being, namely to create creatures on isolated

The frontispiece of the book of organ works written by German music theorist, composer and organist Andreas Werckmeister in the 1690s.

orbs and to allow them to exist for 80 or 90 years, just in order to give them that pleasure, that would be a miserable plan indeed.

[The problem would be, as he put it on another occasion, "shabbily solved".]

Regardless of whether the soul lives for 80 or millions of years, only then to perish, this period is but a reprieve. Finally, it must end. One is therefore forced to the view to which so much attests, even if it is without a rigorous scientific grounding, that in addition to this material world, there still exists another, second, purely spiritual world order, with just as many manifolds as that which we inhabit. In this, you should partake!
—Sartorius von Waltershausen, *Remembrances of Gauss*, p. 103)

For Human Progress, Destroy the British Empire

The following strategic perspective was presented on the LaRouche PAC weekly webcast July 17, which was moderated by Megan Beets. The full webcast may be viewed at the LaRouche PAC website.

Megan Beets: I will ask our institutional question for the evening, which reads very simply as follows: "Mr. LaRouche, how do you assess the deal that has been reached between the P5+1 and Iran?"

I'd like to invite Jeff to come to the podium to address that question, and also elaborate on the broader strategic picture.

Jeffrey Steinberg: Thanks, Megan. we had a discussion with both Mr. and Mrs. LaRouche earlier today.

It was very extensive—it went for over two hours—so it would be impossible to replicate all of the depths of that discussion. But I do want to convey, in response to the institutional question and several other developments, the basic thrust of what we discussed.

Taking for one moment the developments around Greece, and Mr. LaRouche's emphasis on the long arm of the British Empire, which in this case largely worked through German Finance Minister Schäuble: What actually happened is that, over the past few days, the entire trans-Atlantic system reached a potential breakdown moment. Greece did not pay the IMF loans that came due on June 30, but they have only a one-month

Tsipras twitter account

The context for Greek Prime Minister Alexis Tsipras's July 13 announcement of a deal on the Greek debt (left): NATO's deployment in Greece. Here, the USS Truxton is show departing the Marathi NATO pier facility in Greece.

grace period. And of course, this coming Monday, July 20, is the date when a major debt payment to the European Union and the European Central Bank—at least the next tranche of that debt—comes due.

If there was a default by Greece on those debts, then the entire derivatives bubble of unknown, but also massive magnitude, would have blown out; and you would have had an instantaneous collapse of the entire trans-Atlantic and much of the global financial system. That's the point that we're at right now; it's a nightmare moment.

All of the factors driving the world to a war confrontation, are centered around that situation. And quite bluntly, the Prime Minister of Greece—Alexis Tsipras—had a gun to his head. The bottom line is, that he was told that if he went forward and rejected the deal that was being put on the table—a suicide deal—that there would be a NATO coup, and he would be deposed from power. It was literally a gun to his head. And there are people inside the trans-Atlantic intelligence establishment who were well aware of the fact that those were the parameters. The threat was a NATO military coup, an imposition of fascism in Greece, and the beginning of that process elsewhere.

The Nazi Ukraine Precedent

Now, if anybody has any doubts about the willingness of forces within NATO to carry out such a coup, just go back to 2013 and 2014 and the events that occurred in Ukraine. Where the Ukrainian government, the Yanukovych government—legitimately elected, undisputed—was thrown out of power by a neo-Nazi coup with enormous support from within NATO.

Victoria Nuland was the poster girl for that operation, but it was much broader support than that; it was British. So, there was a military coup, using neo-Nazi forces, simply because President Viktor Yanukovych concluded that signing the eastern partnership deal with the European Union would be completely against the national interests of Ukraine. All that's followed from that point, has been a hysterical reaction over the fact that some people in Ukraine decided to act in the interest of their country, and walk away from something that would have been basically the death of the Ukrainian economy and the Ukrainian people.

Ukrainian Embassy of Washington

Assistant Secretary of State for European and Eurasian Affairs Victoria Nuland, with Ukrainian coup leader Andriy Parubiy, in Washington, D.C. February 26, 2015.

So the idea that there was a military coup in the works, and that that was a critical factor in the decision by the Tsipras government to take a rotten deal, is the way to understand that. That will get us very quickly to the larger issue.

You do have, of course, the developments around the intervention on Monday July 13 by Daniel Burke into the Hillary Clinton speech at the New School in New York City, which has, predictably, caused enormous shockwaves across the entire trans-Atlantic region, because the number one issue that the British and Wall Street fear the most—the only thing that they really fear—is that a number of people in critical positions will recognize the bankruptcy of the whole trans-Atlantic system, and will go with Glass-Steagall. That is the solution; there is a solution that is readily available.

There are now Glass-Steagall bills both in the Senate and in the House; in fact, this week a second Glass-Steagall bill, using the identical language of the Warren/Cantwell/McCain/King bill in the Senate, was introduced into the House by some of the very same people who sponsored the earlier bill with Marcy Kaptur, including Congressman Walter Jones. So, the solution is there; it's on the table. It's never a question of whether or not there are available solutions. There are always solutions, no matter how grave the situation, so long as you have a certain kind of human creativity. Looking at the future and coming up with viable solutions. The question is, will there be enough people who show the courage and the historical insight to be able to actually act in a timely fashion?

Now, when we look at the immediate results of the agreement that was reached between the P5+1 countries and Iran, there are many things that could be said. But quite frankly, many of them are quite irrelevant, because we don't know what the consequences are going to be. It's impossible to precisely know them, but it's very important to understand the historical context in which this has happened.

Mr. LaRouche made the point very clearly right at the outset of our long discussion this morning, that you've got to understand the long-wave history of how the empire has operated. And effectively, the Roman Empire never really ended; it changed addresses, it changed names over the centuries. But you've had a system of empire, and in particular, that system of empire was located decisively in the British Empire during two key inflection points in modern history. The more recent of those two inflection points gives you a clear indication of why we can't know precisely what the consequences of the P5+1 deal are going to be, is because of the unknown factors of what might stand in the way of the empire striking back.

JFK Library

In the cross-hairs of the British Crown: French President Charles de Gaulle and U.S. President Kennedy at the Elysée Palace in France, May 31, 1961.

The Empire's Bloody Record

In 1890, you had the British forcing the deposing of Chancellor Otto von Bismarck from power in Germany. And with that one event, the course for war, what came to be known as World War I, and then World War II, was absolutely set in motion. Bismarck was the key factor in avoiding a British-engineered war throughout Europe; and his removal really was the actual starting date of what came to be called World War I.

Now, in the ensuing decade, following the ouster of Bismarck, the British embarked on a wave of assassina-tions. They assassinated President Sadi Carnot of France; in 1901, they assassinated the American President William McKinley. There were, all told, according to historian Barbara Tuchman, over 20 assassinations of prominent individuals that took place in the several-decade period between the dumping of Bismarck and the formal beginning of the fighting in World War I.

That's how the empire operates: provoke wars, provoke confrontation. And at critical moments, select those key historical figures who stand in the way of preserving the power of the empire, and subject them to assassination.

If you continue on past the immediate period of 1890 through the World War I, you see that on a number of critical occasions in history, the British resorted to the mode of assassination. In the 1960s, you had the emergence of a potential trans-Atlantic combination to defeat the power of the British Empire; represented by President John F. Kennedy in the United States, by Chancellor Konrad Adenauer in Germany, and emphatically by President Charles de Gaulle of France. In the sweep of less than a decade, Kennedy was assassinated by the British; the networks that carried out the Kennedy assassination were deeply involved in repeated assassination attempts against Charles de Gaulle of

France, and of other destabilizations that ultimately led to de Gaulle being removed from power before he died.

Those networks were hardcore, Nazi, criminal networks that operated primarily along the border areas between France and Spain. Some of them were literally Nazi remnants from the Second World War; others were part of the French fascist apparatus that dominated France throughout much of its history, going all the way back to the time of the French Revolution and Napoleon. De Gaulle changed that; he established the Fifth Republic, put France on a completely different trajectory. Therefore the British Empire had to get rid of him. And they used neo-Nazi networks, some of which were involved in the French Secret Army operation, some of which were remnants of the Franco fascist apparatus in Spain.

And those were the networks, which were implicated in the Kennedy assassination. They were directly involved in the assassination attempts and the ultimate overthrow of Charles de Gaulle. And, of course, added in the 1960s, the assassinations of Martin Luther King, of Robert Kennedy, of Enrico Mattei in Italy. You had a wave of international assassinations targeting a combination of leaders who represented an existential threat to the existence of the British Empire because they had an alternative policy—one that was based on Hamiltonian American System principles going into the future. You had events like the Apollo program in the United States, that was exemplary of that kind of alternative view of the nature of man and the nature of mankind organized into nation states. You had the 1975 famous linking of the Apollo and Soyuz capsules, which was an historic moment and part of the effort that continued to try to end the Cold War and establish a whole different relationship between the United States and Russia. By that time, the network of leaders from the 1960s had been wiped out.

You had the same thing happen again in the 1980s. Remember that President Ronald Reagan was a close collaborator of Lyndon LaRouche around the project to realize the Strategic Defense Initiative. He was targetted for assassination; he barely survived the assassin's bullets. But the diminished health that Reagan suffered for the remainder of his Presidency effectively opened the door for the Bush apparatus to move in. First, during the Vice Presidency of George H.W. Bush; later, during his

Schiller Institute of Denmark

Deutschebank chairman Alfred Herrhausen greets German Chancellor Helmut Kohl.

Presidency, and after the Clinton period, with George W. Bush. And in effect, Barack Obama has been an extension of the Bush system. So, you had the attempted assassination against Ronald Reagan, a month later, you had the attempted assassination again, also not fully successful, but damaging none the less of the Pope.

And then came the period of the late 1980s, beginning in 1989 at the point that the Berlin Wall came down, and at the point that Germany had a unique opportunity, not just to have a reunification, but to become the key nation in Europe integrating Eastern Europe and integrating Russia back into the community of nations, in the post-Cold War period.

What did the British do? They resorted to a series of targetted political assassinations. The leading banker, Alfred Herrhausen, who was a critical advisor and close personal friend of German Chancellor Helmut Kohl, was assassinated. Soon afterwards, [Detlev] Rohwedder, who was in charge of the re-integration of eastern Germany with West Germany, was also assassinated.

As the result of these two critical assassinations, effectively, Germany was taken over by the British. We see that manifested most clearly today, in the behavior of [German Finance Minister Wolfgang] Schäuble, and in the fact that the largest private financial institution in Germany, Deutsche Bank, became, in the post-Herrhausen, post-Rohwedder, post-Kohl period, an appendage of one of the major City of London British Royal banking groups, Morgan Grenfell.

Germany has lost its sovereignty. And while it still remains a potential economic power in Europe, the behavior of Schäuble, the re-emergence of a Nazi apparatus in Germany, is reminiscent of the British networks around [then Governor of the Bank of England] Montagu Norman, and around American Prescott Bush, which facilitated putting Hitler in power in the first place.

How Can You Judge Current Events?

Without this historical recollection, without this historical knowledge, how can you judge current events? How can you anticipate, and in some cases pre-empt and prevent, the kinds of reactions that we can expect from the British in this particular dangerous, nightmarish, historical moment, if we're blind to history, if we think in "practical" terms, if we don't understand the nature of empire through its long historic sweep?

As Megan mentioned, briefly, you have to also look back at an even larger slice of European history, because it bears directly on the situation in the United States. You had Cardinal Nicholas of Cusa [1401-64], who was one of the giants of the Fifteenth Century, who was really the architect of the European Renaissance. And, when Cardinal Nicholas of Cusa died, the Empire—it wasn't at that point the British Empire; it was the Venetian Empire, and remnants of the Roman Empire, and other centers of imperial power in Europe—went absolutely berserk. To beat back the accomplishments of the Renaissance, including the initial emergence of the system of modern nation-states, and modern political economy, the Empire launched a series of religious wars, that threw Europe into a state of absolute chaos for more than one-and-a half centuries, through the entirety of the Thirty Years' War period.

If you want to understand, and get a real insight into the Hell that was Europe, that was part of the Empire's reaction against Cusa and the Renaissance, then read William Shakespeare. Read his history of the Plantagenets, read his tragedies, and you'll get an idea of what kind of Hell Europe was put through.

But, at the beginning of the Seventeenth Century, towards the very end of Shakespeare's career, you had the emergence of [Johannes] Kepler [1571-1630], and a new scientific revolution, a new Renaissance, was launched in Europe. Even despite the fact that Europe was still going through the hell of the Thirty Years' War.

Soon after Kepler's death, you had another critical figure, Gottfried Leibniz was born [1646-1716]. As long as Leibniz was alive and active, the principles of the scientific revolution of Cusa and Kepler, the principles of the revolution, the Renaissance, and the idea of sovereign nation-states, was prevalent. Quite frankly, the Empire forces were terrified of Leibniz, because he could out-think them on every flank. Leibniz played a critical role in the American Revolution, because he was in the middle of the fight to control the Hanoverian dynasty that moved into the English Throne, during the very beginning of the Eighteenth Century. Leibniz was a key figure influencing circles in the court of Britain's Queen Anne [r. 1702-1714], and a key educator of several people within the House of Hanover, who were earmarked to bring England into a very, very different direction when that German House succeeded Anne to the throne of England.

During that period, a number of critical figures were deployed into North America—key Governors of the North American colonies, who were instrumental figures in shaping the American Revolution a generation later.

The moment that Leibniz died, in 1716, it was the British Empire, that really launched its war against mankind from that point forward. And you had, basically, a war, centered around the American Revolution. The British suffered a defeat in that, quite obviously—a major strategic defeat—and how did they respond? They responded with assassination. The Aaron Burr assassination of Alexander Hamilton was one of the critical events.

Moving forward from there, you had, obviously, a great Presidency with George Washington. You had John Adams, who was part of the tradition, but was weak, had flaws, was limited. And then, from Jefferson on, until the Presidency of John Quincy Adams, you had a British disaster, one after the another. The United States Presidency was effectively recaptured by the British Empire, and it was only the brief four years of the John Quincy Adams Presidency, that pushed back against that factor.

Then, you have to look to [Abraham] Lincoln as the next great figure in American history, who waged war, consciously, against the British Empire, and, through his greenback policy and his commitment to absolute victory in the Civil War, saved the Union, and went back to Hamiltonian tradition that he understood very well. What happened to Lincoln? Assassinated by the British. It was one of the most clear-cut instances of a British-sponsored assassination of an American President that we've had. There were military tribunals that identified the British protective apparatus around the Confederate intelligence services, that were instrumental in the Lincoln assassination.

Fortunately, one of the great Generals of the Civil War, Ulysses S. Grant, was elected President, and did serve two full terms. Of course, his base of operation was New York City. He was very conscious, again, of the Hamiltonian actual roots of the American Revolution.

Then we get to the end of the Nineteenth Century, where William McKinley was the last of the American System Presidents. And, what happened to McKinley? Assassinated by the British in 1901, paving the way for Teddy Roosevelt.

When Franklin Roosevelt was elected President in 1932, even before he was sworn into office, there was an attempt to assassinate him!

President Abraham Lincoln at Gettysburg Nov. 19, 1863, depicted by Fletcher C. Ransom in an oil painting completed in 1938.

When that failed, the J.P. Morgan/London interests plotted an outright military coup d'état, to overthrow Franklin Roosevelt, because of the danger that he presented to the system of empire.

So, you've got a very clear picture, if you're are willing to be courageous enough to step back and learn the lessons of history, appreciate the sweep of history, so that you're capable of devising the kinds of strategic flanks that are indispensable for mankind's survival, going into the future.

The Financial System's Last Legs

Now, we've got to actually have a clear vision of exactly where things stand at the moment, but only from the standpoint of having an appreciation of this sweep of history. The vast majority of our fellow citizens, to put it in very blunt language, are stupid. They don't know this history. They're incapable of judging events like the three dramatic events that occurred just in the last seven days: the intervention with Hillary [Clinton] that shed clear light on where this Presidential campaign is headed; the true significance of what happened in Greece.

In point of fact, nothing was accomplished with Greece. There is no new debt deal. All there is, is a hyperinflationary bail-out of the existing bubble. There is

no way in Hell, that the deal that was struck the other day, can actually last for very long, or succeed in any way, shape, or form. All that happened is that a moment of truth, a moment when the whole trans-Atlantic system was ready to blow out, completely, passed, and it didn't happen. But it's still pending; it's still right there on the surface. Nothing has been done to fundamentally alter the fact, that the British Empire is on its last legs.

Quite literally the British financial system, the London/Wall Street system is absolutely on its last legs, and the persons who represent the British Empire, Queen Elizabeth II and Prince Philip, are thankfully on their last legs as well.

Now, it's very important to look at even the events that have transpired in Germany: Do not in the least, underestimate the importance of the fact that Queen Elizabeth, Prince Philip, and David Cameron were in Germany just in the last several months: They met with Schäuble, they met with Merkel, and from that point forward, the resolve on the part of the Germans to follow British orders, and to move forward with this murderous policy, of killing Greece to save the bubble, has been moving forward.

Glass-Steagall is the absolutely indispensable, immediate step to be taken. Glass-Steagall, under the present conditions, bankrupts the British Empire! It brings down London, it brings down Wall Street, it changes the entire political correlation globally; it lines up the United States, because it finishes Obama as well. Obama is simply there to defend London and Wall Street. If Glass-Steagall is passed, and London and Wall Street are bankrupted, Obama's finished. And that sets the stage for the United States, to accept the invitation by Chinese President Xi Jinping to directly join in the BRICS policy, the "One Belt, One Road" policy, and to make it a truly global alternative.

As Mr. LaRouche emphasized at the end of our long discussion, there must be a positive perspective towards the future. Not just some pollyanna-ish idea, but a very specific, critical, flanking operation, that is feasible and timely and necessary. And happily, we have a countertrend that has begun in the last several weeks, with much work going into it, where a grouping of the members of the United States Senate are beginning to see the bigger picture, and have recognized that Glass-Steagall is indispensable, at this moment.

That's where we are, and this is why it would be really impossible and it would be actually counterproductive to speculate, on the outcome or lack of outcome of the P5+1 deal. Certainly, it's positive that it happened; but with the threat of thermonuclear war, with the threat of the entire dissolution of the trans-Atlantic system as a whole, the British Empire system as a whole, it's really impossible to say how that situation is going to play out, because it's not yet situated in this larger showdown moment that we're living through right now.

Beets: Thank you very much, Jeff. Just to pick up on where you left things, I think the question before all of us, all of our viewers out there, is exactly that issue of human progress. Under this picture that you just detailed, what must mankind do to move forward? And while it's necessary to identify and know the evil which has brought us to the current situation, it's not sufficient. True leadership is the ability to insert into humanity a new principle upon which mankind as a species progresses, moves forward.

As Mr. LaRouche put it earlier: You need to always present a positive force. There are two ways to go: up or down. Up starts with Glass Steagall. Right now. Then you need a science driver program, but you always need a factor that wants it to happen. The key is an increase in energy flux density. If the Obama process continues, we're out of business. We must go back to human productivity. That means a revival of science.

So, with that very simply said, I'd like to ask Jason to come to the podium to address this issue: What do we do to move mankind forward into the future?

The Empire Against the Human Mind

Jason Ross: It's true you can't talk only about the negative things, but I can't resist talking about one more of them, which is possibly the most intense example of stupidity which is expressed in for example the Encyclical of the Pope, *Laudato Si'*, which takes up the British push for reducing the world's population by committing mass suicide by calling carbon dioxide a "pollutant." It's an induced stupidity. It's something that's been created and pushed by Prince Philip, for example, in a very major way, and which is planned to have a major international impact in the conference coming up in Paris later this year, to try to get the world's nations together to sign onto suicide, to agree to goals of carbon dioxide reduction, etc.

I want to contrast the good side of things with a couple of quotes that I thought were particularly revealing from an aide to Prince Philip, Martin Palmer, who's been playing a key role in organizing the Paris conference towards the end of the year, as well as the smaller conference that just took place this month in Paris.

Martin Palmer, this aide of Prince Philip, believes that it is necessary to wipe out the idea that human beings are special, that human beings are the center of creation. He takes particular offense at the notion that man is the measure of all things, and says that one of the problems in creating ecology as a real mass movement, is the resistance that it would find in Christianity, Judaism, and Islam.

Here's a couple of quotes from him [as read]—actually, I'll just read one in particular that I want to come back to. He said, "The pervasiveness of the attitude I am indicating is seen in those elements of the Renaissance that attempted to bring about the elevation of man. The view in these elements is that man is the paradigm of the universe. This is most clearly seen in the drawings of Leonardo Da Vinci. That is what he is trying to depict."

To him, the idea of the elevation of man, man as the paradigm of the universe, that this came across in what Da Vinci had done, and that was the real enemy there. So this was the beginnings of an attempt to really create and push ecology as a religion, starting to be promoted in a very big way by him, in the 1980s.

Let's contrast that with the view that he's attacking,

and go beyond that as well, in looking at what the nature of the human species is, and how progress, as a concept certainly doesn't exist without human beings, and that the notion of purpose for the universe, for ourselves, again, is something that can't exist outside of human minds. The universe itself doesn't have a purpose, independent of us. It would be impossible to try to express one. It couldn't exist; it's actually a notion that has no meaning.

So let's look at these people who are under attack. Let's look at this fight. As we've covered, you know, and we'll get into some amount of detail, there's been a major fight about the role of understanding our relationship to nature: What is the human mind? How does it fit into things? What are human beings? What's our role? You had 2,000 years ago, or a little over that, you had the two differing views of Plato and Socrates, versus Aristotle, where Aristotle said knowledge comes from the senses; the mind is something that gets written upon by experience of the outer world, and that through the senses—touch, in particular, he said, was the best of them—we come to learn things about the world around us. Obviously, we need our senses.

In contrast to that, the view of Plato or Socrates, was that there was something about how nature worked, or better said, there was something about our ability to understand and act in a more powerful way upon nature, that had a connection with the way the mind operates. One of the ways Plato expressed this was with the idea of recollection, that knowledge was always the form of a discovery in a way that felt as though one already knew something and only had to uncover it in the mind. That is, those ideas that are found to be true and have power over nature, and in the arts as well, already exist in the mind and have to be developed or brought forward, that the mind has a connection to nature.

The Renaissance itself was largely created by Cardinal Nicholas of Cusa, as Jeff had mentioned, who had

Top Monarchy operative Martin Palmer (right) and his associate He Xiaoxin at Palmer's Alliance of Religions for Conservation, present an award to His Royal Virus Prince Philip.

developed more work on the nature of the mind, on the nature of discovery, astronomy, medicine, chemistry; he worked in a very serious way in politics and avoiding religious war, unifying the churches. And Cusa's view of the human species was what enabled Kepler to make his discoveries, to throw aside the idea that we could know the world "out there," only as being out there and different from us, but that instead, principles that are of a human nature, such as the principles of music are something that we're going to find out there in the planets; that a notion of cause, of a physical cause that we're able to understand can shape how the planets operate.

So, I think that it comes up in a very concrete way in Leibniz, who—I think this is said about a number of people, but I think Leibniz is one of the most prominent ones—was "the last man who knew everything." Leibniz really did it all: He worked in politics, economics, he made great breakthroughs in science, he developed the calculus, and so on. Leibniz's view was that it was impossible to try to understand nature without using reason as a basis; that the way the mind works is inherently connected with how the universe works.

Vernadsky and LaRouche

LaRouche takes this to another level, where he disagrees with the prevalent notion that knowledge is asymptotic; that we head more and more towards the truth. We never know it, but we're always getting closer and closer and closer. LaRouche for decades has said, "no, that's not the way to understand it." It introduces an error, by separating the human beings who are creating those discoveries, from those discoveries that are supposedly about the world "out there," when in fact, those thoughts that we have which have this power over nature, never actually represent what's taking place in nature, by virtue of the fact that they're never done;

they're never fully right; they're always provisional, they're always susceptible of being overthrown or improved upon, or overthrown in the future.

What it means is that human reason itself is a force of nature, is a power in nature, and that concept is studied in different ways by both the Russian/Ukrainian scientist Vladimir Vernadsky, and the economic work of Lyndon LaRouche. Take Vernadsky first, and we'll end with LaRouche.

Vernadsky studied human beings in a way similar to how he studied life. In looking at life, Vernadsky didn't study individual organisms; he did, but that wasn't his focus. For him, that was the domain more directly of a biologist. What he looked at, was, what is the impact of life as a whole on the surroundings, what does the biosphere itself do as a whole? What does life do? What kind of changes do we see in life as a whole, beyond individual organisms and their functions? What do we see over evolutionary time, with the fact that life moves toward increasing use of energy? And it's those species which participate in that change that survive, and those that don't, which go extinct. And this individual species doesn't participate in that, the evolution as a whole does.

Vernadsky said, look at human beings as a physical phenomenon: What is characteristic of the human species? What is it that makes us human? There's a lot of answers that people have to that. I'm sure everybody watching this has his or her own idea in mind of what it is that makes us human, or makes us different from other animals. I think everyone recognizes that we are different from the animals, even if they're rather not recognize that.

What Vernadsky said, is: look, human beings are the only living species that changes its relationship to nature, that introduces a new kind of time, the time of discovery. No longer are geological ages necessary for changes to take; no longer is evolutionary time, mea-

FIGURE 1

Fuel and Energy Comparisons

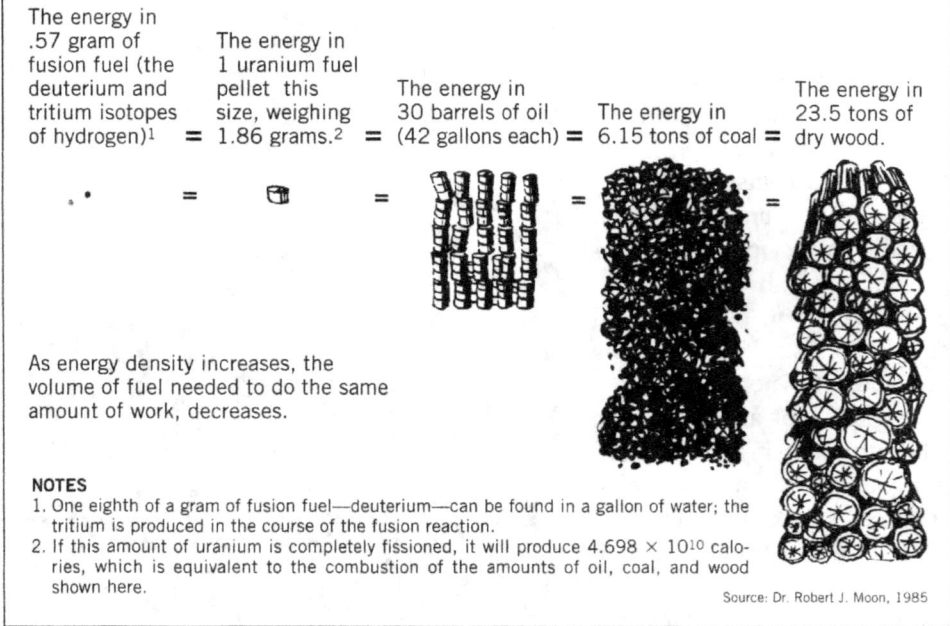

The energy in .57 gram of fusion fuel (the deuterium and tritium isotopes of hydrogen)[1] = The energy in 1 uranium fuel pellet this size, weighing 1.86 grams.[2] = The energy in 30 barrels of oil (42 gallons each) = The energy in 6.15 tons of coal = The energy in 23.5 tons of dry wood.

As energy density increases, the volume of fuel needed to do the same amount of work, decreases.

NOTES
1. One eighth of a gram of fusion fuel—deuterium—can be found in a gallon of water; the tritium is produced in the course of the fusion reaction.
2. If this amount of uranium is completely fissioned, it will produce 4.698×10^{10} calories, which is equivalent to the combustion of the amounts of oil, coal, and wood shown here.

Source: Dr. Robert J. Moon, 1985

The increasing power to do work, as man discovers new ways to increase energy flux density of his fuel supply.

sured in the millions of years, required for the energetic processes of the planet to transform. Now, it takes place on the scale of generations. Now it takes place by action of individuals. Before humanity, individuals don't really exist; there's not any particular significance to an individual jaguar, or a hippopotamus, or anything. Not outside a human relationship to them.

But human beings, individuals, actually matter. Because individuals and societies, make discoveries.

So let's look at how LaRouche measures that. He stressed in the discussion that we had today, the concept of energy-flux density as a guiding principle for understanding progress. Now, I'll just say something briefly about this. I know that many of our viewers might be familiar, but: if we look at the time lines of power that human beings are able to exercise on the world around us, that's changed in dramatic leaps. In the broadest of outlines, we've moved from simple wood, wood fires for cooking food or boiling water, that kind of thing; to the new kind of fire that was created several thousand years ago, by making charcoal. You know you think about this Encyclical from the Pope, where he talks about how the "Earth provides for us"—which isn't true; there are things that we find around us in nature, but the things that we depend on as the human society, increasingly are things that we create ourselves, and that's a measure of our progress, an increasing—not independence from our surroundings, but an increasing power over them in creating our own resources. You might consider the analogy of the move of life from the waters onto land, where you have to bring your environment with you, so to speak.

So what have we done? We've gone from basic wood fire to the creation of charcoal, 5,000 years ago or so; charcoal was necessary to create metals, to create copper, to create bronze, to create, the Iron Age; this was created by resources that we formed ourselves. You then move on to coal—coal, which saved the forests of Europe from destruction. At the time that coal was introduced as a new fuel source, there were serious major deforestation problems in Europe, from wood being cut down for fuel. Coal saved the forests.

Natural gas, petroleum, nuclear power: What we see along the lines of these changes is a *dramatic, incredible*, stupefyingly huge leap! The difference in power that a society using nuclear power has, compared to one with wood fires, isn't of number; it isn't of quantity. It's of quality, it's of kind. It's a different type of power. The processes that we're able to participate in and create, we've transformed. We can control electromagnetism, we have motors,—I don't need to give a list. I think some of these things are pretty direct.

That progress, however, has been stopped, and is directly opposed by this British system. So the breakthroughs of thermonculear fusion power haven't happened, both because of a lack of funding, as well as problems in the scientific outlook being applied to the study of fusion; to the dramatic impacts that the shift from around 1900, starting in the 1890s, since the ouster of Bismarck, the corruption and taking down of culture and of science, especially with the work of logic to replace real science. This has put us in a position where the things that we need to do are necessary, while being incredibly impractical.

And the solution to that, as I think people who are familiar with LaRouche know,—he doesn't take kindly to practicality. That's not one of his characteristics. You have to change what's practical, and we're seeing how

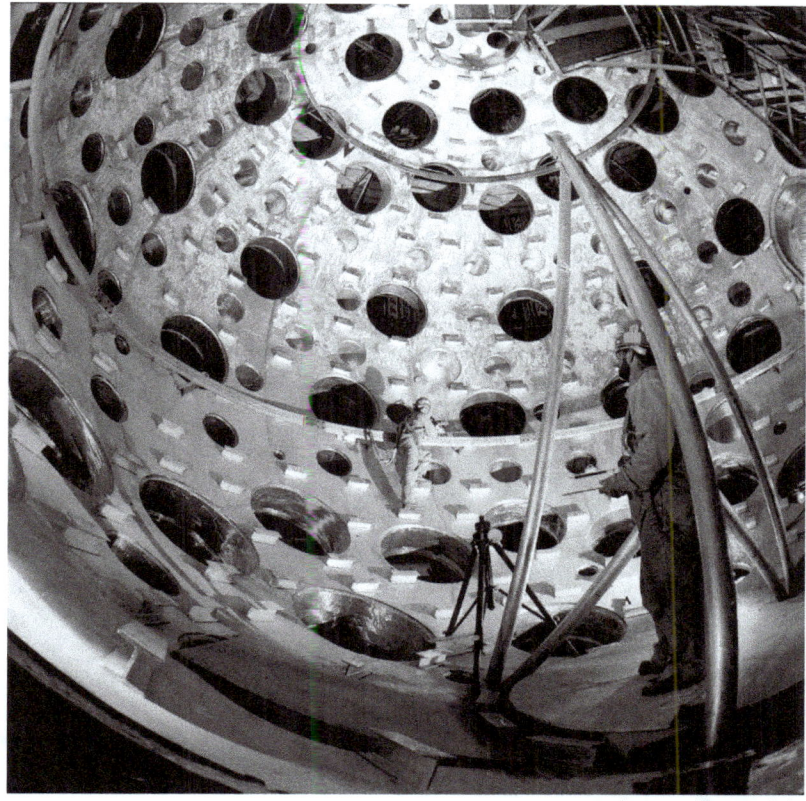

Lawrence Livermore Labs

The unfinished target chamber of the Lawrence Livermore National Lab's National Ignition Facility, one of the U.S.'s few remaining projects for developing thermonuclear fusion power.

this is taking place, how the moves of Mr. LaRouche and his associates have been playing a key role in providing an alternative with the developments around the BRICS, with the new paradigm represented in the global Silk Road, among other concepts; you saw it, for example, with what happened this week, with Daniel Burke putting Hillary Clinton on the spot around Glass-Steagall. That ended up becoming, I think, the first question at the White House press briefing today, where Obama's press spokesman was asked, "Where does Obama stand on Glass-Steagall?" The answer was, "no," in case anyone was wondering.

You change what's practical and that's when you are really being as fully human as you can be. That's how LaRouche acts. Rather than making modest suggestions, we have to have bold demands, an idea of where we're going, and a basis, an understanding, a rooting in history, in science, in culture, to ensure that we have a depth of understanding of where we want to go, of what progress is, to be able to make it happen, to be able to organize it.

We have to dare to be wise, rather than practical.

The Murder of Greece: A Mystery We'd Better Solve

by Paul Gallagher

July 17—The new and brutal cruelties imposed on the Greek nation and people by European "leaders," in the "agreement" reached July 13 created an audible death rattle for Europe. The plan was forced down Greek Prime Minister Alexis Tsipras' throat by blackmail executed over a six-month period, by major international banks and the European Central Bank (ECB), which finally destroyed the Greek banking and payments system and threw the country into chaos. It forced a looting agreement on Greece that will directly seize its infrastructure and banks, impose even sharper tax increases, and wage and pension cuts, and dramatically worsen an economic depression which is already killing and sickening large numbers of Greeks. This, in a country whose public health and hospital system has already almost completely disappeared, after five years of austerity cuts.

July 13 was a day of shame for Europe, said Helga Zepp-LaRouche, who, as Schiller Institute founder, and German stateswoman, has led the campaign to bring Europe into the BRICS-allied nations. The EU now exists only as a monstrous construct, Zepp-LaRouche said in a conference call that day; she cited *Financial Times* senior columnist Wolfgang Münchau, who wrote that "Greece's creditors have destroyed the Eurozone."

The murder of Greece is the death knell for the European Union and for the euro currency zone. Like Greece, other "peripheral members" like Portugal and even Italy have GDPs lower—in absolute terms—than when they joined the euro 15-20 years ago! And their political institutions now know, that if they seek a way to grow while staying within the Eurozone, by restructuring and lowering their debt burdens, they will be murdered as Greece has been. First, international banks will cut off credit lines with their banks; the ECB will then do the same, including to their central bank; and then the slow death by "measured austerity" will be replaced by the brutal slaying of their economies by the "European institutions."

The question remains: What is the motive?

courtesy of Mehran Khalili

On the streets of Athens under the EU dictatorship.

European governments and Brussels "institutions" which carried out this crime, came away empty-handed: The victim had "nothing but the clothes on his back." The ostensible motive was to maintain the sanctity of debt; specifically, the sovereign debts, and sovereign-guaranteed debts, which arose from the swindles which bailed out the big London and Wall Street banks. But the International Monetary Fund (IMF) has produced two reports stating, conclusively, that Greece's 300 billion euros debt won't ever be repaid; and that the new, 86 billion euro bailout loan now planned will never be repaid, either. The creditor perpetrators knew all about these reports, before they were leaked to the public through the media.

The plan, which foresees immediately raising Greece's debt/GDP ratio to at least 225%, perhaps up to 300%, cannot possibly work—except to unemploy, sicken, and kill more Greeks.

The motive of "saving the euro" by keeping Greece in it, is merely the pious posturing of the Obama Ad-

FIGURE 1
Total Population
(millions)

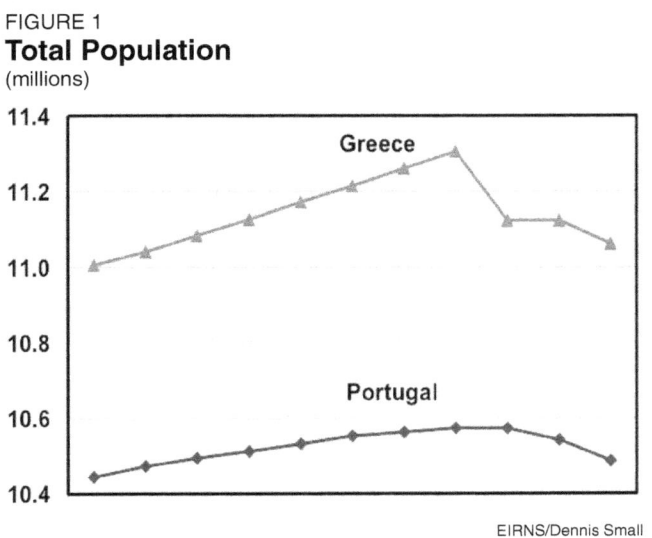

EIRNS/Dennis Small

FIGURE 2
People Experiencing Severe Deprivation
(% of population)

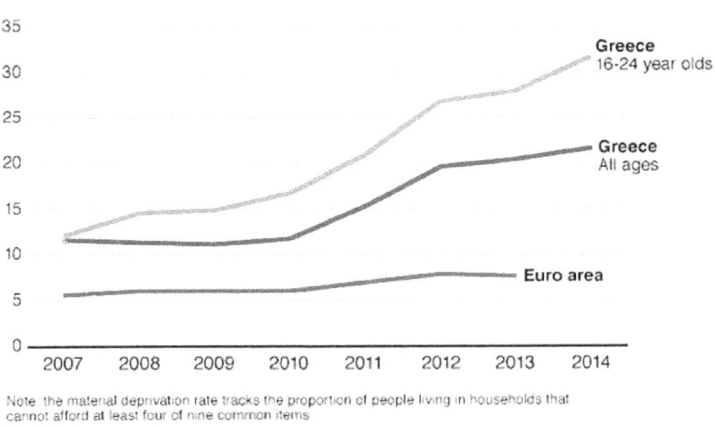

Note: the material deprivation rate tracks the proportion of people living in households that cannot afford at least four of nine common items

Source: Eurostat

Eurostat/zerohedge.com

The category of "severe deprivation" is defined by households living on 12,000 euros or less. The category is roughly equivalent to "extreme poverty" in the United States.

ministration and German Chancellor Angela Merkel. The new bailout loan is likely not to materialize, with the IMF in opposition to it. Greece will default and exit the Eurozone; and in fact, the ultra-right-wing political forces represented by German Finance Minister Schäuble are still demanding "Grexit."

The motive of "teaching a hard lesson" is the only one with legs in the creditor countries, whose media have fanned a rage to punish "lazy, profligate Greeks." But the actual lesson taught to the other "peripheral" countries of southern and eastern Europe—however mum their present governments may be about it right now—is to escape from the euro concentration camp as soon as they dare. The Greek government made such a "Plan B" secretly, according to its former finance minister, but made no attempt to organize Greek deputies or citizens to back it.

The British Empire Factor

What remains, as the motive for the crime, is the *economic austerity, in and for itself, and the resulting depopulation of parts of Europe*. How else to explain the complete support for each brutal austerity measure against Greece, by IMF Managing Director Christine Lagarde, and by the Obama Administration, even as both were warning the European creditor "institutions" that the "plan" could not possibly collect on Greek debt? And the Cameron government in the U.K., which refused to guarantee a single euro-cent of the supposed new bailout loan, but urged on the new austerity measures, anyway?

The European Union will disintegrate; and for what reason?

The accompanying article by Jeffrey Steinberg unravels the thread of the rare and unexplained visit by the Queen of England to Germany and Angela Merkel, June 23-26, just before the "negotiations" with Greece turned into the "catalog of cruelties" described by the London *Guardian*. The British Crown has a long history of wanting populations gone; the Irish in the Nineteenth Century; the Indians under the East India Company and the Empire, for two examples.[1] Here, as Steinberg explains, the geopolitical consequences of London demanding the destruction of Greece—and Schäuble demanding "Grexit"—are extremely serious.

But there are also the London banks, the world center for financial derivatives, featuring that London bank with a German name, Deutsche Bank-Morgan Grenfell. It is the London financial empire which has insisted, since the Ireland bailout in 2009, on "No writedown which touches us, of debt no matter how unpayable, illegitimate, or odious."

The London-centered network of the biggest European banks, along with Wall Street, is exposed to $75

1. See "How the British Crown Reduced Ireland's 'Carrying Capacity' to 6 Million Souls," and "British Colonials Starved to Death 60 Millions-plus Indians. But, Why?" in *EIR*, July 3, 2015.

FIGURE 3
Youth Unemployment in Europe

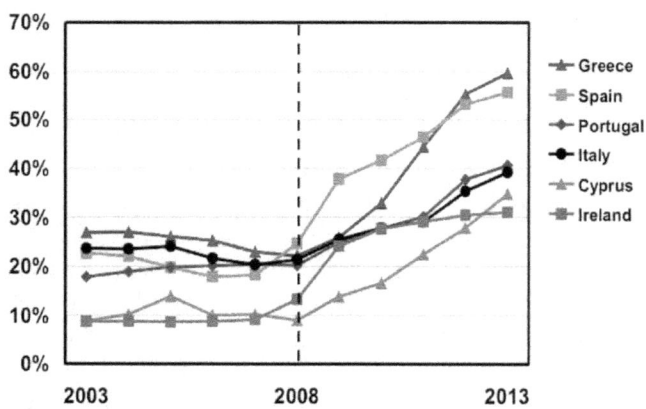

EIRNS/Dennis Small

Available figures in 2014 are not comparable, due to a change in the metrics used by official agencies.

FIGURE 4
Long-Term Unemployment

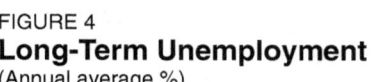
(Annual average %)

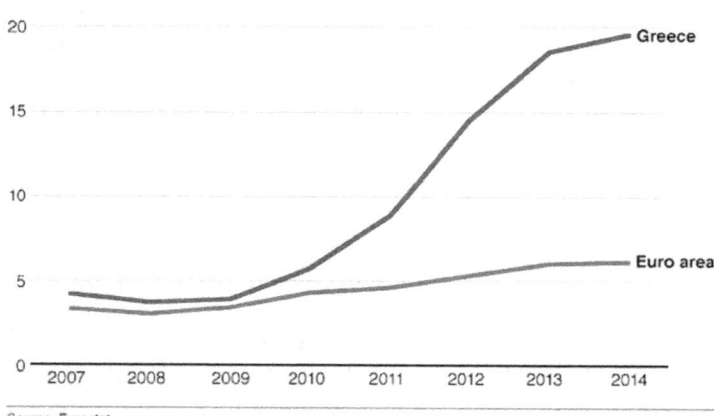

Source: Eurostat

Eurostat/zerohedge.com

trillion in derivatives bets and "swaps" on foreign exchange rates of the euro, dollar, yen, and pound, a $750 billion transactions/day, completely unregulated market. They have exposure to an additional $20 trillion in credit default swaps bets split between London and Wall Street. This is all according to the conservative figures of the Bank for International Settlements end-2014 report.

Any default or significant writedown of debt such as the "Greek" debt, will crush the euro and blow up the banks' foreign exchange derivatives exposure. The credit default swap exposure is another matter, and could make the blowout worse. The bailout debt in the

"European TARP" program known as the ESM (European Stability Mechanism) is over 500 billion euros, created by swindles to bail out the big London-centered banks, and now owed by Greece, Ireland, and a half-dozen other "peripheral" countries. The new loan supposed to be planned for Greece now, would make that nearly 600 billion euros. That debt is largely held by private financial institutions, but guaranteed by so-called "core" EU countries led by Germany. When default actually occurs, these countries are likely to disavow their guarantees, as Austria has recently done.

These same banks, to make their trigger fingers more itchy, have approximately two trillion euros of impaired, mostly real estate-based debts on their books as "assets," including 300 billion euros for the big banks in Italy alone, and 450 billion euros for the French giants.

Even though all these financial powers will "extend" repayment schedules on unpayable debt out to future centuries and other galaxies before they will call out the word "default," the events of July 13 showed that the Union is non-functional, dead. Rather than recovering when "things were settled," the euro started falling, by four cents in the next few days. To quote one consulting firm's "expert analysis" of the Greek crisis: "These movements [of the euro—ed.] are not (yet) as large as those seen in 2007/8. But they are easily large enough to move rates outside the relatively narrow rate ranges seen in most FX derivatives and to trigger increasingly substantial margin calls" on the banks and their financial counterparties.

The motive of the London-centered banks, not to speak of that of the Queen in visiting Germany on that crucial day, is that Greece had to be made a horrible example, that debt is not to be written down—or the banks' derivatives bubble will explode as in 2007-08, but worse.

And in making Greece that example, they lit the fuse to set off that explosion.

The secret of the "Greek crisis" throughout, has been that the London-centered megabanks are bankrupt, despite the massive bailouts which created the debt crises of Ireland, Greece, Portugal, Spain, Austria, etc. These megabanks are drowned in exposure to derivatives losses. They cannot stand for the slightest writedown of debts everyone knows are unpayable—until and unless those banks are put through Glass-Steagall reorganization.

In 1953, when Glass-Steagall bank regulation was in

force in the United States and much of Europe, U.S. and European banks were able to stand the writeoff of nearly 60% of Germany's total debt at that time; this launched Germany's *Wirtschaftswunder*, or "economic miracle."

It's Glass-Steagall now, or murder.

DOCUMENTATION

Greek Parliament Head: 'No to Blackmail!'

July 17—The President of the Greek Parliament, Zoe Konstantopoulou, gave a strong speech during the July 11 plenary debate over whether to approve prior actions for negotiations for a third bailout. Konstantopoulou was one of six parliamentarians to vote "present," a form of abstention, because, as she put it, "the government is being blackmailed to consent to conditions that do not represent it, that do not come from it, that it is struggling to reverse and prevent."

Here are major excerpts:

The Greek people entrusted this government with the great cause of releasing them from the shackles of the Memorandum, from the vise of surveillance and supervision imposed on society under the pretext of debt.

This debt furthermore is illegal, unfair, odious, and unsustainable, as demonstrated in the preliminary findings of the Truth Commission on Public Debt, and as the creditors already knew in 2010. This debt was not incurred as a cyclical phenomenon. It was created by the previous governments through corruption in procurement, bribes, misleading terms, corporate stipulations, and astronomical interest rates, all to the benefit of foreign banks and companies....

After the Second World War, Germany enjoyed the greatest remission of debt so as to allow it to get back on track. This was done with the generous partnership of Greece."

[Today] ... Germany is promoting and enforcing a policy that constitutes a crime, not only against the Greek people, but a crime against humanity....

Ladies and gentlemen,

The artificial and deliberate creation of conditions of humanitarian disaster so as to keep the people and the government in conditions of suffocation and under the threat of a chaotic bankruptcy constitutes a direct violation of all international human rights protection treaties, including the Charter of the United Nations, the European treaties, and even the statutes of the International Criminal Court.

Blackmail is not legal. And those who create conditions that eliminate freedom of the will may not speak of "options." The lenders are blackmailing the government. They are acting fraudulently, since they have known since 2010 that this debt is unsustainable. They are acting consciously, since their statements anticipate the need for humanitarian aid in Greece. Humanitarian assistance for what? For an unexpected and inadvertent natural disaster? Is it an unpredictable earthquake, flooding, a fire?

No.

Humanitarian aid [would be required] because of their conscious and calculated choice to deprive the people of the means of survival, closing the tap of liquidity in retaliation for the democratic choice of the government and the parliament to call a referendum and to turn to the people to decide their own future. The Greek people honored the government that entrusted them, and the parliament that allowed them the right to take their lives and fates in their own hands. With bravery and pride they announced

NO to blackmail.

NO to ultimatums.

NO to the Memoranda of servitude.

NO to the repayment of a debt they did not create and that is not attributable to them.

NO to new measures of impoverishment and exhaustion....

The Greek people are the second to suffer this form of warfare in the Eurozone, preceded by Cyprus in March 2013. This attempt to impose measures rejected by the people in a referendum, using the blackmail of closed banks and the threat of bankruptcy, constitutes a violent overthrow of the Greek constitution and deprives the parliament of the authority granted to it by the constitution.

Everyone has the right and obligation to resist. No resistance in history was easy. But we undertook the popular vote, and we trust the people on the difficult matters. It is to the difficult matters that we must respond. And we must not fear.

This statement was translated by Nicholas Evangelos Levis for AnalyzeGreece! from the Greek text on Left.gr. The full translation is available here.

The Financial System Is Already Bankrupt; The Only Salvation Is Glass-Steagall

by Helga Zepp-LaRouche

July 17—The options for coming out of the crisis for which Greece is only a label, have now been reduced to two: If we continue in the direction that Schäuble, Merkel, Cameron, and Obama have so far marched, a very short-term, complete collapse of the financial system of the trans-Atlantic region will definitely be the result, and will most likely lead to a thermonuclear world war, and with it, the extinction of the human race. The only chance to avoid this unprecedented danger is the immediate worldwide introduction of a Glass-Steagall banking separation law, which, since the introduction of legislation to that effect in both houses of the American Congress, has become a realistic possibility.

Both the murderous agreement which was forced on Greek Prime Minister Alexis Tsipras at the latest EU summit, as well as the so-called stop-gap loan of $7 billion which immediately flows back again to the IMF and the ECB, are pure theater. Because in reality the whole financial establishment knows that the whole banking system of the United States and Europe—the banks, which are allegedly too big to fail, or to have their managements sent to jail—is irrevocably bankrupt. A significant section of this Establishment is only trying to buy time with these measures, and to carry out an anticipated 50% devaluation of the markets—in accordance with the old doctrine of "controlled disintegration," through which it would maintain political control. In the real world, this plan has as much chance of success as the proverbial "snowball in Hell."

In several European capitals people are talking about a Merkel-Schäuble-Cameron axis in connection with this deal. That Schäuble himself is still, even after the EU Summit, talking about a "Grexit" as the preferred option—which has led to considerable irritation in the German governing coalition—is not surprising. The "Europe of two tempos," under which Germany, France, and the northern European states come together as a core-Europe, with total political integration, and the southern European states are practically sent into the desert, has been Schäuble's pet project for a long time. In practice, this plan means a federated state for Northern Europe, under which any possible sovereignty, and with it the consent of the governed, has been thrown out the window, and sacrificed to a Leviathan monster.

To do that, however, the European treaties must be changed, and the assumption, that this would be possible in the face of the total breakup of the treaties in Europe, is a further indication of the total detachment from reality of this power grouping, which has obliterated so decisively and brutally on the "European idea."

The Strangulation of Greece

From the very first day on which the Syriza government took office in Athens, the Troika set in motion a process of strangulation, which could only have one ob-

swiss-image.ch/Jolanda Flubacher
German Finance Minister Wolfgang Schäuble is a "proconsul of the imperial system," charges Zepp-LaRouche. Here he is addressing the Davos World Economic Forum in 2011.

jective: to dispatch this government out of office as quickly as possible, and, to this end, to saddle it with responsibility for all the mistakes which the Troika itself had made.

Among those mistakes were, in particular, the manipulated admittance of Greece into the Eurozone, with the help of statistics which had been falsified by the Wall Street bank Goldman Sachs, as well as the awarding of speculative loans to Greece, which had already been insolvent for five years, and whose banking system was only one of many mechanisms for further ballooning the bubble of the casino economy. Over 90% of the loans and "rescue packages" have not stayed in Greece, but have immediately flowed back into the European banks, which have sated themselves with fat profits, just as the ECB did with its Greek loan purchases, or as the ECB and IMF are proposing to do now with the so-called "bridge loans."

This does nothing for Greece—except to pile up the mountain of debt which has grown in the meantime to somewhere between 220 and 250% of GDP. And if nothing else, that is the reason why the IMF, in a paper which was published by the *New York Times* (among others), concluded that the Greek debt could not be supported, and that it must give a debt "haircut" as well as a 30-year deferral, during which time Greece must pay neither interest nor payments on principal.

A Policy of Empire

What, therefore, is the deeper reason why Schäuble, Merkel, and Co. are pursuing a policy which all the participants know to be unsustainable? A policy, which costs human lives in Greece; which has cut supplies of medicines and equipment to hospitals and as a result caused avoidable deaths; which throws whole families into the deepest poverty and despair; and which leads, in cumulative effect, to genocide against whole groups

EIRNS/Christopher Lewis

Over 90% of the monies the Euro system has "loaned" to Greece has flowed back to the derivatives-stuffed bankrupt European banks, like Deutsche Bank. Here, Deutsche Bank's Frankfurt headquarters.

of the population? A policy which—as whole hosts of international economists and commentators determined after this fatal EU weekend—has destroyed the whole postwar diplomacy, over the last 70 years, of Germany, tying German policy again to that of 1945, and in which the hateful face of the Inquisition, like that Friedrich Schiller wrote about at the conclusion of *Don Carlos*, stares us in the face?

This real source of the crisis is not revealed to those among our contemporaries who see their reason for living in the maximum accumulation of comforts for themselves, comforts which their support for the current system of the global casino economy brings them. These people feel themselves represented best by Merkel, Schäuble and Co., and have developed a remarkable ability to block out everything which might endanger this illusion. In a perfidious way, they have succeeded in killing empathy for the fate of millions of people, and to simply block out the connection between the fast-moving, high-risk finance capitalism of the City of London, Wall Street, and the degeneration of trans-Atlantic culture, as it is expressed, not least, in the increasing violence covered in the media, and carried out in everyday life.

But this cause for the crisis is obvious to those—unfortunately small—numbers of thinking people in our society, who have delved into the long arc of history. Schäuble does not represent the welfare of the European people, and certainly not the German population, but he is the proconsul of the imperial system, into which the EU has avowedly degenerated since the Maastricht Treaty. Such an imperium has emerged in ever new clothing since the Roman Empire: as the Holy Roman Empire of the German nation, as Venetian imperialism, as the Dutch-British Empire, as the Anglo-American Empire, or even as the regional representation of that in the form of the EU.

Hamilton's American System

The American Revolution and Declaration of Independence were established in opposition to this very imperial tradition 239 years ago. In this tradition—the tradition of the American System of Alexander Hamilton—are found the Washington Congressional representatives and Senators who are campaigning for the reinstatement of the Glass-Steagall banking separation system in the tradition of Franklin D. Roosevelt, which, along with the credit system of the Reconstruction Financial Corporation created the preconditions for bringing the United States out of the depression. The reintroduction of the Glass-Steagall law, for which two of the five democratic presidential candidates are openly campaigning, is currently the hottest topic in the United States. The White House has just spoken out against Glass-Steagall in response.

There is a solution to the crisis. The casino economy of the trans-Atlantic Imperium must be shut down. The introduction of a global Glass-Steagall system is the unavoidable first step in that process. Then an international debt conference must separate the illegitimate from the legitimate debts, and write them off. A credit system of sovereign states, as it was envisioned by Alexander Hamilton, must then become the basis for a new international credit system, such as already exists in principle with the new banks of the BRICS states. The European nations must recover sovereignty over their economies and currencies, and then cooperate, as a Europe of the Fatherlands in the sense proposed by Charles de Gaulle, with the BRICS nations in a "win-win" perspective, for construction of a New Silk Road.

In the event that not enough intelligent and moral forces are found to realize this immediately feasible alternataive, the path is unfortunately predetermined: The geopolitically oriented powers of NATO, the United States, and the European Union will escalate their confrontation with Russia and China ever faster, as they see the trans-Atlantic system collapse. The moderization of U.S. tactical nuclear weapons in Europe is good news for all those who want to hook up with a trans-Atlantic ISIS suicide squad.

There is no more time to lose. Glass-Steagall must also be implemented in Europe, now. We have to defend everything against the Schäbles of this world—but above all, our humanity and the humanist culture of Europe.